BOOKBINDING FOR LIBRARIANS

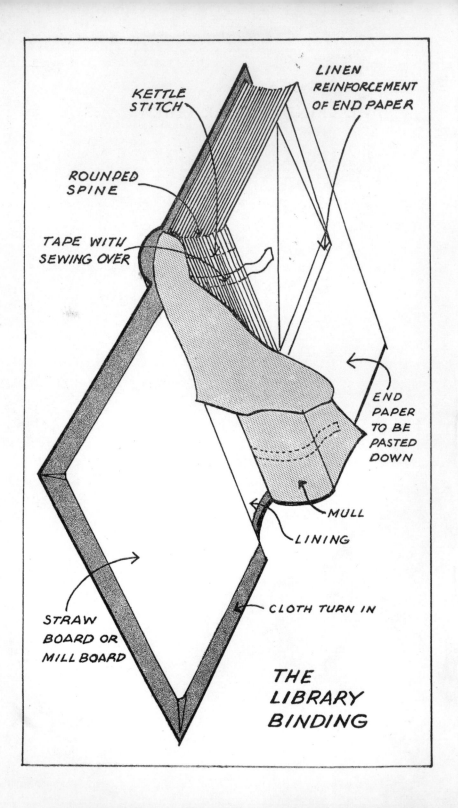

KETTLE STITCH

LINEN REINFORCEMENT OF END PAPER

ROUNDED SPINE

TAPE WITH SEWING OVER

END PAPER TO BE PASTED DOWN

MULL

LINING

STRAW BOARD OR MILL BOARD

CLOTH TURN IN

THE LIBRARY BINDING

BOOKBINDING
FOR LIBRARIANS

by

ERIC A. CLOUGH

Fellow of the Library Association
Deputy City Librarian, Bristol

LONDON
ASSOCIATION OF ASSISTANT LIBRARIANS
(Section of the Library Association)
1957

First published 1957

Set in 11 on 12 point Monotype Garamond.
Printed on Evensyde Cartridge supplied by
J. Dickinson & Co, Ltd, and bound in Great
Britain by Jarrold and Sons Ltd, Norwich.
Book cloth supplied by I.C.I.

CONTENTS

ILLUSTRATIONS

DIAGRAMS

7

AUTHOR'S NOTE

IT IS now more than forty-five years since Coutts and Stephen gave us their *Manual of Library Bookbinding*. Since that time there have been many books published on the craft of bookbinding and a fair amount of material has been published on the history of bookbinding, but little has been written and less published on the practical problems of the librarian who has to deal with bookbinding. The purpose of this book is to fill this gap, and it will be seen, for example, that the chapter on the history of bookbinding concerns itself not with the development of decoration but with the changing techniques and materials used in bookbinding over the centuries.

Inevitably when a book is based on the interpretation of a craft in the light of the needs of a profession some contradictions will arise; some opinions will be given which will not be accepted by both the craft and the profession, and some mistakes will creep in. It is the author's hope that readers who have any comments, criticisms or corrections will write to him so that should there be another edition it will profit from their help.

For technical help I gladly acknowledge the services of Mr. W. A. Floyd, the Foreman Binder of Bristol Public Libraries, the Research Staff of I.C.I. (Leathercloth Division), and Mr. G. F. H. Blunt of Messrs. G. Blunt and Sons to whom I am also indebted for many of the photographs appearing in this book. Mrs. M. Jones and Mr. Peter Heaton have both been of considerable help in the preparation and correction of the typescript, and Miss D. E. C. Salvage and Miss J. C. Cooper have read and corrected the proofs—I am grateful to them. Many other friends in the fields of bookbinding and librarianship have helped with encouragement and advice, and their help is readily acknowledged.

Central Library   E. A. Clough
  Bristol   November 1956

CHAPTER ONE

A brief historical survey of the technique of bookbinding

IT WOULD be amusing but inaccurate to believe that the French librarian who first offered the opinion that "Le lecteur c'est la mort des bibliothèques" was provoked to it by a consideration of the problem of bookbinding. It is, however, beyond dispute that the problems of bookbinding, book protection and book restoration have been an integral part of librarianship from the earliest times. The library in Nineveh—the first known library in our Western civilization—consisted of clay tablets, and these tablets were sometimes covered by earthen jars and attached to the jars were tags giving the contents. Doubtless the librarian seven centuries or more before the birth of Christ pondered on whether he could afford to cover his books with special cases—did the value of the contents justify it or was the use such that it required additional protection? These are the two questions that from that time on were to perplex librarians.

We have the great library of 400,000 manuscripts at Alexandria under the Ptolemies, where not only were the literary treasures of classical civilization acquired and stored but also where the magnificent collection of books produced at Alexandria itself was kept. There can be little doubt that it was at Alexandria that we first come across an example of organized book production followed by systematic storage and exploitation.

But if we are to concern ourselves with the actual craft of binding books we must look back no further than the fifth century A.D. and the Byzantine Empire for the first real evidence of binding books as we understand it. This late flowering of the Roman Empire was to produce work displaying all the symmetry and discipline of classical times and yet combine with it the mysticism of the East and extravagant decoration of the Near East. Whether the final product was a miniature ivory or St. Sophia at

Constantinople, the Ravenna mosaics or the church of Holy Luke in Greece, all the finest work displayed that synthesis of the East and West which makes it fascinating to both civilizations. The lovely metallic Byzantine bindings with their jewelled insets and ivory cameos are now all collection pieces and, incidentally, many have had the misfortune to be separated from the works they were originally designed to protect and many more are forgeries. It seems appropriate, too, that the craft of bookbinding should also have flowered in Spain under the Moors as leather work had long been an established craft amongst the Arabic peoples. That it did so flourish cannot be doubted by anybody who studies the illustrations in the late Sir Henry Thomas's *Early Spanish Bookbindings* in which work he states that the Royal Library in Spain in the early eleventh century consisted of 400,000 books.

Of Ireland it could truly be said that at no time has that country come under the influence of either the Moors or the declining Byzantine Empire, and so it is without any clear link that we must move to Ireland for our next stage of the journey. The link may be explained by the *cumdach*, which is a specially ornate box-like cover for a sacred book or books which was produced in Ireland in the ninth century A.D. with elaborate hammered silverwork and inset jewels. Bindings similar to these *cumdachs* or shrines can be found in the ancient churches of the Greek Orthodox Church, and there is little doubt that there was a two-way traffic in skilled craftsmen and artists between the Continent and Ireland. Certainly the links between the Emperor Alexius and the Anglo-Saxon people were real enough. The actual Celtic bindings were perhaps never so exquisite as the superb manuscripts of the eighth century A.D., including the *Book of Kells*, but from the fragments preserved in the various museums in Eire it is clear that these bindings were Byzantine-like both in their design and the materials they used as they were covered with gold and silver and inset with jewels.

Such a step forward brings us to the monasteries, for it was in the monasteries that the production of books was almost entirely centred from the fall of Rome to the thirteenth century. It would be quite inaccurate to give a picture of a large number of wealthy church establishments devoting their time and energies to book production and bookbinding. There were certainly a large number of monasteries and abbeys which produced and bound a number of books for their own and occasionally outside use. Some small abbeys produced a number of crudely bound missals which have a certain charm, but it was the principal religious centres of St. Albans, Canterbury, Durham, London and York that established a national and at one time an international reputation for the books they produced and bound. For six centuries throughout civilized Europe books were written, bound and distributed by the monasteries. Subsequently the decline of the influence of the monasteries and the development of the universities resulted in some changes in the organization of book production, but the techniques of bookbinding established and developed in the monasteries is the basis of all subsequent binding, so that today the hand techniques are clearly related to these early methods. Accordingly it is this early method of binding that must now receive our attention.

THE TECHNIQUE

The material used for the production of books in the monasteries was vellum, and in the sewing of the manuscript sheets the obvious development from the earlier codex is apparent as the sheets were produced in pairs of conjugate leaves and were usually made up in quires of quaternions or four leaves. These quires or sections were stitched to each other and to folded strong strips of vellum or leather which were laid at right angles to the fold of the quires. The strips of leather or vellum were then threaded through two wooden board covers and the end of the strip pegged down. Over this exposed piece of book machinery a piece of leather was occasionally pasted down over the back and over such part of the boards as was necessary to cover the laced-in strips or thongs, and in this way the early quarter-bound book was produced. The boards were heavy and strong for they were designed not only to protect a work of considerable value but also to serve as a permanent press for the vellum, which otherwise would have curled. To these boards were added further protection in the way of metal bosses, metal clasps and chain holders. The finished book was usually of considerable size and weight—the vellum and the heavily decorated oak or beech boards produced a work which could not be comfortably read other than on a reading-desk or table, and the often repeated story of Petrarch having been in danger of losing a leg because it had been damaged by a book falling on it could well have had a sound basis in fact.

The spine of a monastery-bound book bears a striking similarity to the book produced "in boards extra" today. The sewing was made by passing the thread in and out through the centre of the fold of the spine, round the vellum strip or folded cord and then over the headbands at the head and tail of the book, and so on to the next section without interruption until the book was fully sewn together. The headbands were thus a vital as well as a decorative part of early bindings, and they were used to reinforce the joint between book and boards by fastening the overlapping headbands diagonally across the top inner covers of the boards and finally threading them through holes in the boards.

The handing over of the technique of binding to the printer-publisher was to produce modifications in many aspects of the technique and in the materials of binding. It was found that if the book was to be trimmed at head and tail, or, as was more often the case, just the head, it was then necessary to stop the sewing short of the head and tail, otherwise the sewing would have been trimmed off and the thread broken. This was achieved by introducing a linking stitch or kettle stitch with the previous sections to fasten the sections one to the other. After the book was trimmed the headband could be added in such a way that it lay decoratively but uselessly inside the head and tail edges of the spine. The headbands ceased to be made of plain linen thread twisted round a piece of cord, but often became a carefully designed coloured band of either linen or silk threads. Again it was found by such printer-publishers as Aldus Manutius that instead of flat vellum strips cords could be used. The use of these cords created a fundamental change in the shape of the spine of the book in that the cords gave the appearance of raised bands, and these bands varied in number from three to six, depending on the size of the book. The majority of books subsequently bound in Europe carried raised bands until Thomas Mahieu some seventy years later restored the fashion of using flat vellum strips, and occasionally binders subsequently encouraged the practice. In the seventeenth century the deplorable practice was introduced of recessing the cords by sawing slots in the back of the books at the folds into which the cords fitted and over which the sewing thread passed.

The thread used in early sewing was a fairly fine linen thread which varied slightly in colour and texture from country to country, but it was used without a break, so to speak, until the eighteenth century when occasionally fine silk thread was used. It seems to be generally agreed in spite of further experiments by Cobden-Sanderson in the nineteenth century that silk is an unsatisfactory thread for book sewing because it lacks the grip of linen thread.

The basic construction of these early bindings had a number of defects. One of them was that the sections tended to "start" or move away from the spine so that the fore-edge became uneven and was consequently subjected to excessive wear. The second defect was that there was nothing other than the cord or vellum lacings to hold the boards to the back of the book—and subsequently there was a rough covering of leather, but neither was adequate for a heavy book and inevitably the cords were strained and stretched so that the boards often slid back away from the fore-edge. Once again the printer-publisher came to the rescue, and with the increased production of books came rounding and backing. These processes are more fully described in Chapter 5 as are all the hand processes which have been carried down the centuries to contemporary practice. Rounding and backing are designed to hold a book together so that it keeps its shape and opens easily. This is achieved by rounding the spine and so giving a crease to all the pages at the back edge of the book and bending the pages over away from the centre. In this way opening the book is facilitated and the pages are locked together. At the ends of the curve given to the spine the process of backing gives a turned-over lip to the spine so that boards fit snugly on the book and are also held in position.

About the time of the introduction of rounding and backing also came the introduction of lighter boards to replace the heavy wooden boards. The board most frequently substituted was pasteboard, and this was made by pasting together sheets of paper from the printing shop. It was found that this strong but light board was quite sufficient for the smaller paper books, and it has also served, quite by accident, to preserve evidence of the early printing of books which would otherwise have been lost to us.

A book is bound when all the leaves are sewn together in such a way that they become a unit. To this fundamental unit there have gradually been added boards; covering materials for the boards; lettering on the covering material; protection for the covered boards and lettering and design for that protection. It has taken us one thousand five hundred years to reach the point in the advancing technique of bookmaking where we are now considering plastic jackets for the protecting material on the covered boards.

THE COVER

The early monastic binders produced books for use and they must soon have realized the obvious advantages of strong boards which protected the valuable products of their scriptoria, and they almost as quickly realized the need for some protection of the spine. Certainly the early medieval covering material consisting of the tanned skin of the cow, sheep or deer was simply a piece of leather pasted down over the spine and part of the front and back boards. The leathers used cannot be firmly associated with any particular country, but it is true to say that goatskin is usually associated with the early Spanish bindings, and pigskin was widely used in Germany.

The advance from quarter-binding to whole-binding was a logical step which took place fairly quickly, and with the improvement in the tanning and finishing of the skins of both wild and domestic animals, there was produced on the boards of a book a fairly smooth attractive surface which provided an obvious vehicle for decoration and subsequently for lettering. In England the leather most widely used was calf; many books were bound in rough suède like deerskin and pigskin; but generally speaking the early English binders coming after the monasteries established a tradition of using soft, smoothly finished calfskin. Occasionally they used the stronger, harder skins, but their finest work was done in soft skins, and of these the rarest and the most beautifully grained was the skin of the guinea deer.

It was this use of calf which provided such an admirable opportunity for the use of stamps and rolls, and although it would seem that many European countries discovered these techniques at about the same time, there can be little doubt that the English and French decorated bindings of the period are the first examples of this type of craftsmanship. Not that the use of these tools represented the first use of decoration on bookbindings. Many centuries earlier, as we have already seen, we had the beautifully extravagant Byzantine bindings with their precious metal covers, studded with jewels. The use of enamelling had also been mastered in the Byzantine Empire, and this together with the inlaid ornamental pattern as used by the masterly Moorish craftsmen were almost certainly introduced into Western Europe by the Crusaders.

But to return to England and the manuscript or printed book bound in full calf and decorated with blind stampings. Mr. J. B. Oldham and the late G. D. Hobson have given a good deal of thought to the development of blind stamped panels on English bindings, and readers are referred to their published works for a detailed study. Here it should be sufficient to note that the development of the roll whereby the binder could impress a sequence of designs by applying a wheel with the design engraved on the circumference to the leather opened up a new field of design and book decoration in the sixteenth century. A more fundamental change introduced at about the same time was the use of the panel stamp, and to use this the binder needed to expand his technical equipment by the addition of a strongly made blocking or arming press. When it is realized that prior to the introduction of panel stamping all binding had been carried out by means of small hand binding tools it will be seen that this was indeed a revolution which was to divide the craft into those who carried out *la reliure à petits fers* and *la reliure industrielle et commercielle*. These panel bindings were produced by fastening the engraved metal or wood to a block which could then be fitted into the press and applied by pressure to one book after another.

The use of gold as a medium for decorating and finishing was probably first introduced into Spain by the Moors in the fourteenth century or even earlier, and from there it travelled to Italy, where it was certainly in use in Naples in the late fifteenth century.

Surprisingly its advance into other European countries was slow, and not before the seventeenth century do we find the art of impressing gold-leaf on leather bindings widely used in Germany, France and subsequently England.

With the development of this simple medium to reinforce the use of blind tooling and stamping, the technique of book decoration made considerable headway. It is no part of this short survey to consider the development of the various decorative techniques which are used to distinguish one material or even individual binding style from another. It may nevertheless be of interest to examine very briefly the use of gold-leaf as part of the finishing process in early binding.

Anthony Koburger, of Nuremberg, was one of the leading printers and stationers of the fifteenth century, and he bound his books in an elaborate and distinctive manner, but more important for our particular purpose he printed the title of the book in gold upon the top of the obverse cover. With the introduction of panel stamps the practice of lettering the book titles on the covers seems to have fallen out of general favour for a time as the booksellers exercised their ingenuity with elaborate coats of arms.

The names of many of the distinguished bookbinders, printers and patrons of book production are known and have received acknowledgement from both scholars and students, but it must be remembered that from the beginning to the end of the sixteenth century the printer or stationer was usually the binder, and he bound such copies as were likely to be immediately required and then sold them to the public if he was registered as a bookseller. Subsequently the work of binding was carried out by master binders under the direction of the stationer-bookseller. Certainly until the advent of Grolier bookbinding was largely a commercial task carried out by means of blind and subsequently gold-stamped work. It is at this early stage that we have the use of the stationer-bookseller's device—the equivalent of the publisher's device of today. In the Plantin-Moretus Museum can be seen an example of the printer-binder's device—the familiar circle describing an arc with the motto "Labore et Constantia".

These commercial bindings developed and showed the influence of the various artistic developments of craft binding down through the centuries, but the fundamental pattern and procedure was not to be changed until the Industrial Revolution brought cheap power, and with it came the mechanical casing machine, and cloth covers. So little did the craft change that it would be true to say that the binding of a book in boards extra by a bookbinder today would readily be recognized by a bookbinder of the sixteenth century as a technique with which he was almost completely familiar.

The introduction of cloth in place of leather as a covering material came in the nineteenth century, and this was fairly soon followed by the mechanization of the craft of binding. Power-operated machines quickly debased the gentle tradition of bookbinding and gave us that Victorian monstrosity, the cloth cased book with the fully lettered and more than fully illustrated cover which rarely fails to astonish us with its concentration of illegibility and poor taste on one small piece of cloth.

Fortunately the debased design of the cloth-covered book was rescued in the early part of the twentieth century, not so much by the influence of William Morris or the craftsmanship of Cobden-Sanderson and Douglas Cockerell as by their colleagues in the printing and publishing trade, such as Pickering and Whittingham, who had in the previous century carried forward the tradition of disciplined printing into the design of a disciplined commercial binding.

Today the design of publishers' cases has acquired a dignity and a sense of design which promises well for the future and serves as a tribute to the much maligned publisher and his typographer. Certainly it is foolish to lament unduly the fact that the binding and design of a book have changed more fundamentally in the past hundred years than in the previous six hundred years. Such a change has probably brought with it the collapse of the craft of handbinding, but in return thousands of books are produced in place of the small edition produced for the occasional scholar, or the sumptuously bound book for either the prince of the Church or State.

CHAPTER TWO

The raw materials of
bookmaking and bookbinding: paper

To THE making and binding of a book are brought a large number of ancient skills, complex machinery and a wide range of materials. The materials and skills have not changed greatly in the past five centuries, and it is understandable why the printer, the publisher, the librarian and the book buyer, having seen the results of their predecessors' efforts, tend to be rather conservative in their approach to new methods. But we live in times of considerable change, and throughout this book an attempt has been made to face up to the use of new techniques and materials in the hope that as a consequence a critical but sympathetic approach will be brought to these techniques and materials by all who are concerned with bookmaking and bookbinding, and that this in turn will enable books to be produced more cheaply, more plentifully and more tastefully.

Although not actually a part of casing or binding, the paper used in a book is the basic medium upon which the binder works, and it inevitably plays a considerable part in any decision reached by the librarian as to whether a book shall be bound or not. It follows that a consideration of the making of paper, the use of paper in making a book, and the various types and sizes of paper is essential if the full process of bookmaking is to be understood.

Paper consists of a thin mat of flexible cellulose fibres with added filling material and colouring matter. These cellulose fibres come from a wide variety of raw and manufactured materials, ranging from cotton and linen rags to esparto grass and wood. The strength of the fibre is basically related to the length and diameter of the fibre, and as these range from 0·06 (straw) to 1·033 (cotton) inches in length and 0·0005 to 0·001 inch in diameter in the normal machine-made paper, it will be seen that there is a considerable strength range. The process to which these fibres are subsequently subjected inevitably affects the strength of the finished paper, but no treatment, however painstaking, can give strength to the paper made from straw, which has a fibre with an average length of about six hundredths of an inch.

Cotton and linen rags provide the raw material for the finest grades of paper, and they are today rarely used other than with an admixture of cheaper materials. The rags are cut up into lengths and boiled with a bleaching agent. After softening, cleaning and bleaching, the pulp is well washed and fed into a beating machine which breaks down the material to a fibrous mass without substantially breaking down the fibre lengths. It is at this stage that other materials are added and may consist of pulps made from other materials; or chemicals and dyestuffs to give the paper its finished characteristics; or of sizes, starches and fillers to give the finished paper a smooth hard surface.

Until comparatively recently most of the printing-papers used in book production contained esparto grass which was imported largely from North Africa and Spain, but the steady increase in price has forced British paper manufacturers to use straw and other substitutes for this grass, and it seems likely that with the development of new processes a good deal of book paper will contain straw fibres rather than grass fibres. The treatment of both materials is, however, indistinguishable for our purposes.

The grass is first cleaned and is then boiled and softened after which it is washed again and broken down into fibres prior to bleaching. The pulp is then treated according to the type of paper it is intended to produce. For example, the fine-grade imitation art papers are usually made of an esparto grass base with a 30 per cent loading in order to fill up the interstices of the fibres and produce a high gloss finish suitable for half-tone blocks, but quite unsuitable for binding. Esparto usually produces a lightness and bulkiness in the finished paper, and this is offset by mixing it with anything from 15 to 40 per cent sulphite wood pulp.

Wood pulp is the principal raw material used by the paper-maker, although its use in book paper is not so considerable as it is in most other types of paper. The woods that are used are largely soft conifers of which spruce is the most satisfactory with a fibre length of about one-ninth of an inch, but deciduous woods

19

are also used, including those produced from chestnut and birch. Unlike esparto the pulp is usually imported as such, and this pulp has been made in the country of origin by the usual process of cleaning, breaking down and shredding into a fibrous mass. There are two types of wood pulp, chemical wood and mechanical wood. Mechanical wood is made by grinding the logs on a rough stone—a process which inevitably breaks off the fibre length and leaves a good deal of non-cellulose material, with the result that papers made from this material lack strength and deteriorate quickly on exposure to normal atmospheric conditions. It is essentially a cheap basic material for the manufacture of wrappings, poster papers, newsprint and the like. It is as newsprint—which contains 80 per cent mechanical wood—that it presents a problem to both librarian and bookbinder.

Chemical wood is a material which is greatly superior to mechanical wood, as it is produced by a variety of chemical processes which have in common the treatment of the wood by boiling it under pressure with a chemical which helps to ensure that the fibres are separated from the non-fibrous material without any marked reduction in fibre strength. It is, inevitably, a more costly process than that used for mechanical wood, and the relative values of these two types of raw material can be assessed from the fact that whereas in chemical wood 50 per cent of the basic raw material is used for paper making, in mechanical wood 90 per cent is so used.

The various pulps are combined with the appropriate chemicals, and the mixture is then passed on to the stuff box, which is the reservoir tank feeding the paper-making machine, or to the vat if the paper is to be made by hand.

A rag pulp is normally used for a hand-made paper, and the process for making such paper is expensive and slow. A vatman dips his sieve-like tray into the vat of pulp and nicely judges the amount of pulp for a single sheet of paper. The pulp is then shaken from side to side in such a way that the fibres mat with each other, and in this way hand-made paper is given its two most marked characteristics in that the thickness of the paper varies slightly from sheet to sheet and it has no grain, being equally strong in both directions.

The paper-making machine, on the other hand, controls the thickness of the sheet so that it varies only within the narrowest limits, but such a machine cannot quite imitate the twist and shake of the skilled vatman's hand, with the result that machine-made papers have a grain or a direction in which the fibres tend to run, thus giving the paper a weaker resistance to tensile strain across the direction of flow of the machine.

Both hand and machine processes have in common the method of supporting the fibrous pulp in water and then drawing the water off as the fibres are shaken down and matted together. Inevitably in such a process the bottom part of the paper web contains a lower percentage of long fibres as compared with the top part of the web, and these fibres are neither so well matted nor so well filled at the bottom of the paper. The result is that all paper has a top surface that is relatively well matted and filled and a bottom surface that is relatively open grained.

From all this it will be seen that the fibre from which the paper is made controls not only the basic strength of the paper but also in a machine-made paper it is responsible for grain or directional strength. The grain of a paper is an important quality in a well-made book, so it is desirable that the paper for a book should be folded in such a way that the grain runs with the fold and not across it. This apparently illogical use of the strength of the paper is because paper folds easily along the grain, and if a book is made with folds across the grain it will not lie flat and opens stiffly.

The direction of the grain in machine-made paper may be detected most simply in a laid paper by identifying the laid lines or wire marks which always run across the direction of the grain of the paper. In a wove paper it can be ascertained by folding, and it will be found that the fold along the grain gives a much sharper fold than the fold across the grain. A more conclusive test is by damping a piece of paper on one side, and it will be found that if the dampened side is placed face downwards the paper will curl and the valley of the curl lies along the direction of the grain. The reason for this is that moistened paper fibres expand up to 30 per cent in diameter, but only 1 per cent in length.

The relative humidity in which paper is stored controls its behaviour, and although the variations in sizes of paper brought about by varying storage conditions cause particular difficulties to the lithographic and photogravure printer, it also presents some problems to the bookbinder and the bookmaker.

The paper trade today is increasingly conscious of the need for research into new materials and new techniques. The British Paper and Board Industry Research Association plays the leading rôle in this research and gives encouragement and support to the research sections and laboratories established by the principal paper manufacturers.

Paper is manufactured in a large range of varieties and under a bewildering array of trade names with the result that similar papers by different makers carry quite different names, and it certainly cannot be assumed that a similarity of name indicates a similarity of paper. The manufacture of book paper is a fairly specialized section of the industry, and the paper produced falls into the two categories of laid paper and wove paper. Laid paper carries laid lines or wire lines which can be seen by holding the paper up to the light, but in the case of machine-made paper these laid lines are contrived quite artificially and have no real significance other than as a means of ascertaining the grain of the paper. Wove papers, on the other hand, have an even structure and no markings are visible when it is held up to the light.

A hand-made pure rag paper has a body, a surface and a crispness that make it a pleasure to handle and a clearness of colour and texture that make it a delight to see. Well printed with a good black ink, it establishes a link with the earliest printers and book-makers, and can serve as a vehicle for the display of the highest qualities of craftsmanship. Such paper is extremely strong, being made from a raw material with a long fibre which is subjected to a minimum of chemical processing. That it is extremely durable can be demonstrated by the examination of books printed more than five hundred years ago on such paper.

Machine-made rag paper or mould-made paper has according to some experts the same lasting qualities as a hand-made paper, and this may be so, but the variation in strength through the direction of the grain seems to make such a claim unreasonable. Certainly such a paper—and it is rarely used other than for limited editions—has the visual appeal of the hand-made rag paper.

India paper or Bible printing is an extremely thin (0·0018 to 0·0022 inch), but remarkably opaque paper and the better qualities are made from hemp; but as with most high-grade papers it has been found that a mixture of processed chemical wood serves almost as well. This fine paper is not particularly suitable for library use as the pages are frequently rather difficult to turn over and the books swells so much on binding that it is difficult to round satisfactorily.

Featherweight paper lies at the other extreme of the paper-maker's art as it has considerable bulk and little substance. The real featherweight has gone out of fashion except for Bumper annuals for children, but the fluffed-up, uncalendered esparto grass fibres continue to be used to provide a bulky paper for the publisher who wishes to sell his books by size rather than by quality. Inevitably such a paper with its loose texture is a most unsuitable medium for binding as the paper soils quickly and the thread cuts through the paper it is intended to hold.

Antique paper covers most of the papers used in the making of books today. Like most widely used terms, it has been corrupted so that it means little other than a paper that has not got a smooth well-calendered surface. Many of the antique papers are quite strong and have a pleasant surface that carries print extremely well. This paper is also widely used for printing books containing illustrations using photogravure or offset lithography.

Calendered paper is quite unlike antique paper in that it is given a polished surface by hot rollers revolving at different speeds, and the paper itself usually carries a fair amount of loading. It is a paper which gives pleasure to the printer of half-tone blocks, but its lasting qualities seem to be impaired by the strenuous processes to which it is subjected, and this together with a slightly unpleasant appearance makes it an unsatisfactory book paper.

Art paper is a paper made from a fine fibrous web which receives a heavy coating on both sides of china clay. This coating is pressed and glazed so that the finished surface is smooth and suitable for the high-grade reproduction of fine screen half-tone blocks. Of all the papers used in bookmaking this is the most unsuitable from the bookbinder's point of view. It is particularly vulnerable to damp or excessively humid conditions. When sewn the paper breaks down and when guarded it tends to separate the coating from the web; most unsatisfactory of all is when it is used for tipped-in single plates.

Imitation art paper is a poor relation of art paper. The glossy appearance is not quite so strongly marked nor is the paper quite so white and the difference in manufacture is that this type of paper is made by loading with china clay, barium sulphate or chalk in the early stages of the process.

Imitation art if well made is a much superior paper to its superior relation real art paper, as the fibrous strength—such as it is—runs through the body of the paper, and the loading can, up to a certain point, serve to give strength to the finished product. The intelligent printer and publisher reserve the use of such paper for the reproduction of fine screen half-tone blocks.

Cartridge paper is a heavy-weight antique with a fair amount of sizing and considerable strength. It is not often used for books other than those printed by the offset process, but it provides an admirable medium upon which the bookbinder may exercise his craft.

Kraft paper, usually a strong, glazed, brown wrapping-paper, but as with many terms in the paper trade it has been corrupted so that it now also means a bleached, white, unglazed paper. It is, nevertheless, a most versatile paper, being occasionally used in binding as a lining paper on the one hand and as a backing paper for a laminated book jacket on the other.

Tissue paper. A light-weight paper used for repairing books. The best grades are made from rag and other fibrous material.

Parchment. The term is now usually used to mean the various types of paper intended to imitate the parchment skin. The nearest imitation is *parchment substitute*, which is a strong, off-white, deckle-edged paper used largely for legal documents. There are also vegetable parchments, oiled parchments and glazed imitation parchments.

Such a list represents merely a sketch of the various papers used in bookmaking, but it would be true to say that most of them fall into one or other of the various types listed. Certainly it would be unwise to lay down an ideal specification for a paper which would serve for all books for all time. The Library Association's recommendations based on those of the Royal Society of Arts are now quite out of date and unrealistic. A book paper must be selected for the purpose it is destined to serve, and the majority of books are intended for use and not primarily for preservation for posterity. The paper-maker's search is for a long-lasting and cheaply made paper, but with the advance of scientific knowledge in paper-making it follows that the ideal paper for a particular book is not a matter for a permanent specification.

The size of books is related to the size of the paper from which the books are made, and the following sizes are the most frequently used for writing and printing papers.

Description	Size of sheet	Folded once Folio	Folded twice Quarto	Folded three times Octavo
Foolscap	13½ × 17	8½ × 13½	6¾ × 8½	4¼ × 6¾
Crown	15 × 20	10 × 15	7½ × 10	5 × 7½
Large post	16½ × 21	10½ × 16½	8¼ × 10½	5¼ × 8¼
Demy	17½ × 22½	11¼ × 17½	8¾ × 11¼	5⅝ × 8¾
Medium	18 × 23	11½ × 18	9 × 11½	5¾ × 9
Royal	20 × 25	12½ × 20	10 × 12½	6¼ × 10
Imperial	22 × 30	15 × 22	11 × 15	7½ × 11

It will be seen that to describe a book as a folio, a quarto or an octavo gives no clear indication of its size as it will be seen that an imperial octavo is larger than a crown quarto. The format merely serves to give a rough idea of the shape of the book unless the format is linked to the paper size.

It would be misleading to give the impression that book papers are actually printed in these sizes. Today they are almost invariably printed on multiples of these sizes such as double demy, 22½ × 35 inches, or quad crown, 30 × 40 inches.

CHAPTER THREE

The raw materials of bookbinding: cloth, leather, leather cloth

CLOTH WAS first used for edition binding in the early part of the nineteenth century, and it subsequently became the conventional covering material for all cheap books other than those that were paper covered. It is not known who first introduced this material into the process of bookmaking, and certainly it came at a time when edition binding was already being cheapened and mechanized to cope with the increased flow of books and the practice of publishing such books in paper covers was by then firmly established. Its introduction must have appeared to many to be a retrogressive step and one which continental publishers refused to take then or since. Subsequently the development of the technique of blocking the cloth-covered book was to bring about towards the end of the nineteenth century as degraded a piece of design as even the Victorians could contrive. The aim was to cover the cover with a large illustration which was supported by wreaths of ivy tendrils and a title which, if it was not particularly legible, was clearly distinguishable because it was carried in a florid panel and consisted of curiously distorted letters. In spite of this, the introduction of cloth-covered cases was to serve well English publishing and, incidentally, English librarianship as it helped to produce a hard-wearing, well-made and, subsequently, well-designed book.

Today cloth comes next to paper as the most important material in bookbinding. A wide range of cloths—one American manufacturer issues a catalogue giving nearly one thousand different strengths, grainings and colour combinations—together with substitute cloths have overwhelmed the competition once offered by leather, and cloth is today used for all types of binding and casing work.

A fairly recent development has been the manufacture of a

waterproof, oil-resistant cloth which is now widely used for library binding, and this is also produced in a wide variety of colours and grains. Although it is claimed that some of these cloths can in fact be washed, it would seem to be an unnecessary refinement for the average home reading library where the qualities of such cloths are valued because they are reasonably stain and rain resistant.

The quality of the cloth is based on the strength of the original cotton cloth and this ranges from the open weave light quality fabric used for the cheapest type of publisher's casing to the double warp closely woven cloth used to make buckram. The basic strength of a woven fabric can be very roughly judged by the number of threads per square inch, and the American Library Association minimum specification for class A library binding lays it down that there shall be at least 110 threads per square inch.

The process of making this cloth is the same as that used in the manufacture of a wide variety of unfinished cotton fabrics. The raw cotton is ginned as a result of which the hair-like fibres are separated from the cotton seed, the twigs and the dirt, and the clean fibre is then baled for export to the country where it is to be spun. It is subsequently cleaned again by blowers, combed into a rope-like sliver which is then twisted and pulled on the spinning machines until the required yarn size is achieved.

Individual threads of yarn are then wound on to a large roller called a beam, and these threads form the warp of the finished fabric. Each warp is a continuous piece of twisted cotton up to twelve miles in length, and the number of such warps is an important factor in the wearing qualities and strength of the cloth. These warp yarns pass through a device which raises alternate threads, or pairs of threads in the case of double warp fabrics, and the shuttle containing the weft yarn passes through the threads as they are alternately raised and lowered.

The woven cloth is known at this stage as grey cloth, and it is this type of cloth which is acquired from the weaving mill by the manufacturers of bookbinding cloths.

The desizing, cleaning, bleaching and washing of the cloth are carried out in a series of elaborate processes which produce a white cloth in varying widths, but usually in rolls varying between

1,000 and 2,500 yards in length. The cloth is carefully inspected, and uneven pieces produced by badly spun thread or with breaks or tears are removed and the cloth is then cut off into the required lengths.

Most conventional cloths used in bookbinding are dyed to the finished shade before they are filled or coated. There are, however, a number of bookbinding cloths known as white-backs which are available in a fairly wide range of colours and these are not so treated. The purpose of filling and coating is to give the cloth a body which will resist the penetration of the glue and which will occasionally give it a body and an appearance of strength which it does not possess. The treatment of ordinary cloth and water-proof cloth differ from this point. The ordinary cloth is filled and coated by squeezing the dyed paste into it several times by means of heavy rollers, and then calendered to give the required surface gloss and grain. It should not be assumed that such filling is deleterious as it would seem that a filling of up to 20 per cent gives added strength and serviceability to a well-woven cloth, but a poorly woven cloth with a heavy filling quickly deteriorates under bending and friction and releases the filling before it breaks down. The fillings used in finishes of a non-waterproof type are usually made from a starch base, with the result that they are remarkably susceptible to heat and moisture. Water, exposure to rain, or use as a teapot stand all result in a white stain being made, and the higher the finishing content the more susceptible it is to such staining.

Before the last war the leather cloth which was occasionally used as a substitute for leather in large bindings was coated with a nitro-cellulose and castor oil filling, and this gave it both a distinctive smell and an almost imperceptible tackiness characteristic of leather cloths, but considerable advances were made immediately before and during the last war in the development of synthetic resins, with the result that there are today a wide range of processes for the manufacture of leather cloth and oil-proof and waterproof bookbinding cloths. In this country nitro-cellulose continues to be the most widely used, but among the more frequently used plastics, particularly in the U.S.A., are thermo-setting polyvinyl butyrol, polyvinyl chloride, improved types of nitro-cellulose and ethyl-cellulose, cellulose aceto-butyrate and a range of synthetic rubbers. The application of all these materials to cloth has been accompanied by the development of appropriate plasticizers. These coating media are mixed with the required pigment and then either spread over to form a coating or diluted and pressed into the fabric, which is subsequently passed through a drying machine where the solvents are dried off, leaving a flexible as well as an oil, stain and water-resistant surface. As with the ordinary bookcloth, the waterproof cloth or leather cloth is embossed in order to give it the required finish by subjecting it to considerable pressure under heated and engraved plates or rollers. The plates or rollers used for this process can produce many attractive and ingenious designs, but they tend to result in a fairly clearly marked break in the design at frequent intervals. The cloth is then finally checked and the bookcloth, which is usually 38–40 inches wide in the case of conventional cloth, or 48–50 inches wide in the case of waterproof cloth or leather cloth, is usually made up into rolls 30–36 yards long and dispatched to the bookbinder, but special rolls of leather cloth are produced in 100-yard lengths.

What qualities are we to look for in a finished cloth, and what improvements can we reasonably hope to see in the near future?

Essentially the cloth must be manufactured in a wide range of colours and qualities, and it should be improved by an attractive finish. It must be easily worked and lettered by either machine or by hand, it must keep its shape, colour and texture, and it should be reasonably priced, although it should be recognized that cloth is not the most costly item in the binding of a book. A demy octavo can be bound in a medium-weight waterproof library cloth at a cost for the cloth alone of 3½d.—the cheapest cloth would cost 2d. and the best quality buckram would cost 5d. The best of these cloths would almost certainly be made of cotton and would probably have a double warp to give it strength; certainly such a cloth would be free from imperfections, particularly in the spinning and weaving.

If we look to the United States for our standards we find that according to the minimum specification for class A library binding approved by the American Library Association the cloth used in such bindings has to weigh not less than 7–9 ounces a square yard; the total thread count, including warp and weft, is to be not less than 110 threads per square inch, and the tensile strength (by the strip method) is to be not less than 120 pounds per inch for the warp and 70 pounds per inch for the weft, and not less than 200 pounds per inch for the sum of warp and weft.

It would be foolish to draw any detailed conclusions from the figures shown in the following tables, which give an analysis of the wearing and soiling qualities of various specified cloths used for bookbinding. The sample is small, the books were all octavos, and the terms used for the classification are not sufficiently specific, but the aim was to divide the specimen books into three categories which would roughly represent the classification used by librarians in a home-reading library. *Slight* in this case signifies that the book is marked with wear or dirt, but fit for a good deal of further use; *moderate* is used to indicate that the book is to be allowed to return to circulation if the actual text is still fairly fresh; *considerable* is used to indicate that the book is only fit for immediate withdrawal. The books were divided into the various categories by an experienced, practising library bookbinder.

AN ANALYSIS OF THE WEARING AND SOILING QUALITIES OF VARIOUS SPECIFIED CLOTHS USED FOR BOOKBINDING

Washable medium leather cloth
LB2   Imperial Chemical Industries

Number of issues	Number of books	Wear			Soiling		
		Slight	Moderate	Considerable	Slight	Moderate	Considerable
5– 9	2	2	—	—	2	—	—
10–14	6	6	—	—	1	5	—
15–19	6	6	—	—	2	4	—
20–24	6	5	1	—	—	5	1
25–29	6	6	—	—	3	2	1

Washable medium cloth
Celdek   K. J. Scott

Number of issues	Number of books	Wear			Soiling		
		Slight	Moderate	Considerable	Slight	Moderate	Considerable
5– 9	3	3	—	—	2	1	—
10–14	5	5	—	—	4	1	—
15–19	7	7	—	—	3	4	—
20–24	4	4	—	—	3	1	—
25–29	7	7	—	—	5	2	—
30–34	7	1	5	1	3	2	2
35–39	6	4	2	—	3	3	—
40–44	6	5	1	—	3	3	—

Art canvas
Not washable   Winterbottom

Number of issues	Number of books	Wear			Soiling		
		Slight	Moderate	Considerable	Slight	Moderate	Considerable
5– 9	2	2	—	—	—	1	1
10–14	—	—	—	—	—	—	—
15–19	—	—	—	—	—	—	—
20–24	4	3	1	—	—	1	3
25–29	2	1	—	1	—	1	1
30–34	3	2	1	—	—	1	2
35–39	4	2	1	1	—	2	2
40–44	4	2	2	—	—	—	4
45–49	5	3	2	—	—	2	3
50–54	6	2	3	1	—	2	4

Single-warp buckram
Not washable   Redbridge

Number of issues	Number of books	Wear			Soiling		
		Slight	Moderate	Consider-able	Slight	Moderate	Consider-able
5– 9	—	—	—	—	—	—	—
10–14	3	3	—	—	—	2	1
15–19	8	3	5	—	—	3	5
20–24	5	2	3	—	—	2	3
25–29	10	6	4	—	1	6	3
30–34	6	4	2	—	1	4	1
35–39	11	9	2	—	1	6	4
40–44	4	—	3	1	—	2	2
45–49	4	1	3	—	—	1	3
50–54	5	2	3	—	1	1	3

Washable heavily coated cloth
Arberlave   Redbridge

Number of issues	Number of books	Wear			Soiling		
		Slight	Moderate	Consider-able	Slight	Moderate	Consider-able
5– 9	—	—	—	—	—	—	—
10–14	—	—	—	—	—	—	—
15–19	3	3	—	—	—	3	—
20–24	1	1	—	—	1	—	—
25–29	3	3	—	—	1	2	—
30–34	4	—	4	—	1	1	2
35–39	3	2	1	—	1	2	—
40–44	2	1	1	—	1	—	1
45–49	2	—	2	—	1	—	1
50–54	1	—	2	—	—	2	1

Book cloth—unwashable

Winterbottom

Number of issues	Number of books	Wear			Soiling		
		Slight	Moderate	Consider-able	Slight	Moderate	Consider-able
5– 9	—	—	—	—	—	—	—
10–14	3	2	1	—	2	1	—
15–19	6	3	2	1	4	2	—
20–24	2	1	1	—	2	—	—
25–29	3	3	—	—	1	2	—
30–34	1	—	1	—	—	1	—
35–39	3	1	1	1	1	2	—
40–44	5	2	—	3	—	3	2
45–49	2	—	1	1	—	2	—

The conclusions that might reasonably be drawn are: (i) books bound in conventional cloth are more frequently withdrawn because the cloth is soiled than because they are worn out: (ii) washable cloths are most suitable as they soil less quickly than non-washable cloths and wear better; (iii) a medium-weight washable cloth with a smooth finish not carrying a great deal of filling is probably the most satisfactory for octavo books. It should be added that the most suitable cloths have tended to be marketed in a limited range of colours until recently, but a new range of attractively designed light-weight leather cloths is now also available.

There seems no occasion to ask for a book cloth exactly according to the A.L.A. specification, but it cannot be doubted that there is plenty of scope for the British bookcloth manufacturers to raise their standards so that a more closely woven washable cloth is generally available, and such a cloth should be available in a wide range of colours and finishes.

Of the substitutes for cloth the best known is probably *Linson*. This consists of a fairly strong fibre base rather like uncalendered paper. A filler is well pressed into the fibre and then calendered and given an appropriate grain. Laboratory tests would seem to demonstrate that this substitute material is as strong as cloth from the point of view of standing up to folding and creasing, but a book cover is subjected to more than folding—it is rubbed, it is knocked and it is pulled. Such strains when carried out in the library itself would seem to show that such a substitute cloth is not quite so strong as a conventional cloth, but a careful examination of publishers' cases covered with this material has demonstrated that a slim crown octavo book may stand up to nearly sixty issues. Out of a sample of five hundred books the conclusion was that the average life of a case in such material was 80–85 per cent of the life of a cloth-covered case.

PATRA (Printing and Packaging Allied Trades Research Association) is at present engaged in an investigation into the wearing qualities of book-covering materials, and the co-operation of a number of librarians should ensure that the report will be of interest to publishers, binders, librarians and bookcloth manufacturers.

LEATHER

The pleasure of seeing and handling a book bound in leather is unequalled. The sight and smell of a row of books well bound in leather has such a fascination that today one of the most lucrative sidelines for the second-hand bookseller is the sale of sets of leather-bound books as so-called library furniture. Such books are bought not to be read but to look well and are a development of that tiresome shelf of books which consisted only of false backs.

Leather handles well and finishes well, but in spite of the efforts of propagandists it does not appear to wear as well or last as long as cloth. It may very well be that the leather of today if suitably protected will have a reasonably long life, but compared with cloth the cost is high, and it would be sentimental to overlook the experience which can be gained by the careful examination of the stock of any large library that has been binding books for the past three-quarters of a century and has on its shelves books bound in the last three centuries.

The processes used in converting the various animal skins into leather are designed to improve the appearance, increase the durability and enable them to be readily used. These processes have often resulted in the leather being left with an acid content, or more usually have rendered them susceptible to the absorption of sulphur dioxide from the atmosphere. Such an acid content inevitably produces a rapid deterioration or rusting of the leather, and as a result of the research of Dr. Plenderleith of the British Museum and PIRA (Printing Industries Research Association) it would now seem that leather may be adequately protected for a time by treating it either during the manufacture or subsequently with a solution of potassium lactate, and details of such treatment are given later in the chapter on the repair and care of books.

Today the process of manufacture has been modified by the more reputable firms to meet the recommendations of the Royal Society of Arts as laid down in their final report of 1905. These recommendations were that there should be no use of over-strong tanning agents; that the dyeing solutions which incorporate acid to produce a bright even colour should be avoided; that the over-scraping and splitting of skins should not be carried out; and that care should be taken to avoid the complete removal of the natural grease in the skin.

Probably the most widely used leather today is *morocco*—a term which when used correctly applies only to goatskin. This attractive leather has a long fibre and a clearly marked grain which is often exaggerated by false graining. It is supplied in skins of varying qualities and varying sizes, and the most satisfactory is the hard-wearing beautiful leather known as *cape goat morocco*. A more widely used variety is *niger morocco*, which is a product of both Nigeria and the Mediterranean where it is usually tanned and dyed, but the crudeness of the native flaying results in tears and holes being made in most skins. When it is known that a skin will often be irregularly shaped and only include three to four square feet it will be seen that these imperfections make such skins expensive. Many other good quality moroccos are supplied from various African and European countries, and practically all of these leathers are grained artificially by pushing and pressing the surface in a board after it has been soaked and softened. The various grain finishes—the best of which is probably small grain—add pliancy and improve the appearance of this useful leather. There seems little point in the occasional practice of giving a marked false grain to the leather.

Pigskin or *hogskin* is reputed to be a hard-wearing, attractive but rather thick and inflexible leather which has considerable strength if correctly processed and left undyed or only lightly dyed. It is easily recognized by the distinctive triangular groups of small holes caused by hair or hair cells. Unfortunately this leather loses its strength when pared, and as it is usually produced in large undamaged skins it is obviously more suitable for such work as newspaper binding, where the heavy joint needs little paring.

Sealskin used to be frequently recommended and occasionally used for reference library binding some thirty years ago, and there is no doubt that this attractively grained but rather oily leather has lasted extremely well. It is rarely used today, being both expensive and rather difficult to "finish", but nevertheless, Douglas Cockerell used it occasionally with great success, and it is one of the three types of skin produced in accordance with the PIRA test.

Of the wide range of leathers that remain—and it should be remembered that all animal skins including human skin can be tanned and processed into leather for bookbinding—the best known is *sheepskin*, and when carefully processed and not subjected to an absurdly heavy graining this soft leather is reasonably durable and pleasant to handle. *Basil* is probably the most widely used variety of sheepskin and its lightly grained surface together with its range of soft brown colours result in it occasionally being used for the recovering and rebinding of old books. In spite of this it is a material which does not meet with the approval of many craftsmen.

Occasionally librarians and binders have experimented with the use of brightly coloured split sheepskins known as *skivers*, but their attractive colours and ease of finishing are more than offset by their short life—a life which is too short even for the nonfiction title with a limited life and only receiving occasional use in the home reading library.

Calf has a beauty, a smoothness and a delicacy of appearance that is often associated with the skins of immature animals; unfortunately it must also be recognized that all leathers from immature animals lack durability and most of the books which can be seen on our shelves in rusted and collapsed bindings have been bound in calf.

The cost of leather together with the imperfections and the irregular shape of the various skins have left an obvious market for imitation leathers and leather cloths. With the development of plastic fillers and the various felted fibres made from cellulose waste, imitation leathers have been produced and are now being marketed and used fairly widely. They tend to be rather thick, but so far as limited experience will allow such a judgement they appear to be hard-wearing and stable. The cost is 8s. 7d. a square yard as compared with, say, 6s. a square foot for niger morocco.

The best-known substitute for leather is leather cloth, and today this is widely used for bookbinding and is made in a wide range of qualities, shades, grains and other finishes. The surface of leather cloth can be sponged over and it is fairly stain-resistant. It is readily blocked and printed, and the finished book both looks and wears well. It suffers from the disadvantage of being a little clammy to the touch and its adhesion, although generally adequate, is not as good as the conventional binding cloths.

CHAPTER FOUR

The raw materials of bookmaking and bookbinding: thread, glue, paste, tapes, board, gold and foil

THREAD

Whether the thread is continuous as it is in hand sewing, or consists of a number of separate threads as it does in machine sewing, it is a fundamental part of the making of a book, and when consideration is given to the strain imposed on the sewing in the normal handling of a volume of newspapers weighing anything up to 30 pounds it will be realized that the thread used in bookbinding must be both strong and durable.

It can be manufactured from cotton, linen, silk and nylon. Cotton thread should be evenly spun without knots and it is manufactured in varying thicknesses or reels for the various types of sewing machine. Although it is bleached (and bleached thread is supposed to have a short life), it would seem that most reputable firms remove any bleaching agent which is likely to produce rapid deterioration. It is, and has been for close on a century, the most widely used thread and serves admirably for machine casing and conventional library binding.

Linen thread is superior to cotton thread in strength and durability. It is not usually bleached and is sold in hanks by the pound. Thickness varies from No. 12, which is rather like a fine string, to No. 30, which is the finest, and suitable for most books unless they have a large number of particularly thin sections.

Silk thread was popularized by Cobden-Sanderson, but the general opinion of hand binders by whom it has been used would seem to be that it is difficult to handle as the maintenance of a steady sewing tension cannot be achieved without a great deal of practice and there is a tendency even in the highest grade work for sections sewn in this way to sag. Nylon thread is today being used occasionally by publishers' binders, and it has such striking advantages over other materials that it seems certain to be more

38

widely used in future. Unlike cotton it maintains a perfectly smooth knot-free surface and is stronger than cotton. It has the considerable advantage of being cheap and it can be manufactured in finer grades so that books can be more easily nipped, rounded and backed after sewing as the swelling caused by the sewing is not excessive in the case of thin paper editions. Its principal disadvantage appears to be that it contracts, and when the books are cut apart the nylon thread tends to slide back, and so loosen the end sections. Technical production difficulties have also tended to slow up its use, but there seems every possibility of this new synthetic thread becoming the normal material for sewing a book.

More recently Terylene thread suitable for sewing machines has been introduced and is now available in small quantities. It has the advantages of nylon and does not have quite the same high degree of elasticity, with a result that the problem of thread pulling back after cutting is overcome.

In choosing a thread for a book, whether it be for a publisher's casing or a hand-sewn extra binding, the thickness of the thread chosen must be related to the thickness of the paper and the number of sections. A thread that is too thin will not give a sufficient swelling at the back to enable the book to be effectively rounded and backed. One that is too thick will produce a book that is too swollen at the back, and this will produce difficulties in nipping, rounding and backing, resulting in a tendency to produce creases in the inner margins and a poorly shaped back.

GLUE AND PASTE AND OTHER ADHESIVES

During the past twenty years the joining together of surfaces by means of adhesives has been the subject of considerable research, and out of that research has come a new industry with a wide range of adhesives. The uses of adhesives are endless, and the laboratories attached to the factories are responsible for the careful balancing of the various qualities in an adhesive to ensure that it is suited for each new task or each new variation of each new task. It is now possible to put a house together in large sections by means of an adhesive; it has certainly been possible to laminate a wing for a high-speed aeroplane by means of adhesive for the past fifteen years or more, and the strips of a carpet to make up the conventional rectangle are frequently fastened together by means of an adhesive. How does all this affect the bookmaker and the bookbinder?

It would not be surprising to find that the traditional craftsman had largely rejected such scientific advances, but in fact the adhesive maker's skill has been widely used, so much so that even animal glue has been considerably modified and is produced now in a large number of varieties for particular classes of work and particular machines. Nor have the synthetic adhesives been neglected, and there can be few factories where books are bound and cased that have not modified their techniques to take advantage of recent developments.

Glue has been known and used since the time of Ptolemy, but its use on a commercial basis in our Western civilization only dates back to the eve of the seventeenth century. The effect of the new industry on English craftsmanship was most striking in the revolution it brought about in the manufacture of furniture, giving us the airiness of Sheraton for the heaviness of Jacobean. In bookbinding the effect was neither so striking nor so immediate, but it was ultimately to enable the bookbinder to produce a more serviceable, a better shaped and not quite such a cumbersome book.

There are four basic types of glue, and they all have in common the fact that their adhesive qualities arise from the collagen in the bone or skin of the animal or fish.

Bone glue. Glue of a sort can be made from the bones of any animal, but practically all bone glues are made from large cattle bones and the inner bony structure of hoofs, the outer surfaces of which, contrary to the popular idea, do not in themselves yield any glue.

Hide glue. These are made from the parings removed by the tanner when he prepares the skin, and these consist of the head, tail and legs and occasionally the scrapings from the soft underside of the skin. This hide glue gives us the finest and strongest glue used in the book trade.

Rabbit skin glue. This is a high-quality material made from the defurred pelts—the fur is used incidentally in the making of the finest type of felt hats.

Chrome glue. This is made from the trimmings of chrome leather —ordinary leather trimmings cannot be used—and makes a light-coloured easily worked glue, but it is not so strong as hide glue. A light coloured glue is usually supposed to be a superior-glue, but in fact the colour is no guide whatsoever except that a really light glue has probably lost some of its strength in the bleaching process it has been subjected to.

All animal glues used in the making and binding of books are now the so-called flexible glues, and this quality of flexibility ensures that the possibility of books cracking and breaking down the spine as they would if they were bound with untreated glue and then carelessly handled has been overcome. Originally this flexibility was gained by the use of glycerine as an hygroscopic agent, but nowadays there is a wide range of cheap but effective substitutes for glycerine such as sorbitol and glycol. In addition the modern glue usually contains some such chemical as para-nitro-phenol to make it resistant to attack by bacteria and finally a chemical is added to reduce the offensive smell of the heated glue.

The finished product is then marketed in a fairly wide range, depending upon whether it is for general use, or for casing work, or for use in a gluing machine.

In the workshop it is essential that the glue should be carefully treated. The heating process which makes the glue fluid must be gently carried out without exceeding 150° F., and a thermostatically controlled heater should be used to ensure that this is done. As glue is an organic material it soon becomes sour if subjected to frequent reheating, and as this sourness is produced by bacterial action it follows that sour glue quickly contaminates fresh glue, and it is thus very necessary that all glue-pots, brushes and machines should be thoroughly cleansed and scraped at regular intervals and certainly should be so treated before a new pot of glue is heated up.

The resinous adhesives are today challenging the use of glue in a number of bookbinding processes. These adhesives of which the best known is *polyvinyl acetate* are used for unsewn binding and for case-making, particularly when the case is made with a

41

waterproof cloth which inevitably presents difficulties if the conventional glue is used. This particular adhesive is usually made by suspending polyvinyl acetate with a plasticizer in water, and when dry it gives a transparent but strong adhesive film of excellent bonding qualities. It is now used, for example, with an added anti-fungicide, for the mounting and preservation of maps coming into the custody of the Clerk of the Records in the House of Lords.

There are a great number of synthetic resin adhesives marketed today, but it would perhaps be appropriate to conclude by mentioning one that appears to offer tremendous possibilities for the bookmaking and bookbinding trade. The *hot-melt* adhesives are being developed rapidly in the United States, and research is being carried out by one of the largest chemical combines in that country. Hot-melt adhesives have similar thermoplastic qualities to glue in that they become liquid and easily workable at a low heat, and set almost instantaneously on being reduced to normal temperatures. It is, of course, the speed of setting which gives them such potentialities for modern bookbinding machinery.

Paste has been used for centuries in the making of books, and today its slow setting, non-staining qualities ensure that it is still widely used. The functional difference between the use of paste and glue hinges on the speed of setting, and where a careful adjustment of surfaces is called for the slow-setting paste or a slow-setting synthetic adhesive is commonly used. Where a quick firm set is required on the spine of a book, for example, then glue or something similar is used.

Many of the early pastes and more particularly those used in the seventeenth and eighteenth centuries were often rather coarsely made with the result that today the endpapers have often come away from the boards, and the brushmarks used to lay this inadequately cooked paste are still there to be seen. Such pastes are of interest to those engaged in bibliographical detective work, as it is possible to distinguish the fairly recent pastes by the additional chemical content, because as with glue the manufacturer today adds additional chemical pastes to act as fungicides. Certainly modern pastes do not contain the fine grains of stone which can be found in the earlier flours ground by millstone.

Today the bookbinder can obtain his paste from a wide variety of products, ranging from the prepared white commercial paste to the chemical-free starch powder used for high-grade binding and in specialized processes such as the fixing of silk gauze to the surface of documents.

To enable paste to be used with treated cloths a solvent in the shape of diethylene glycol is occasionally incorporated. A recent and most interesting development in the United States has been a modification in the making of paste introduced by the Government Printing Office in order to overcome the warping of book boards produced by the expansion of endpapers when moistened with paste, and the subsequent contraction as they dry out after being fastened to the boards. It was recognized that the moisture content was responsible for the problem, and it was accordingly decided to reduce the water content and introduce glucose as a substitute solvent. The paste now used is made up as follows: water added at the start 35 per cent; diethylene glycol 10 per cent; beta naphthol 0·1 per cent; alum 0·3 per cent; glucose 20 per cent; flour 19·6 per cent; water from condensation of steam 15 per cent.

GOLD

The gold-leaf used by the bookbinders of today ensures a glowing, clear-cut and durable finish which is superior to that produced by any other transfer material. The use of gold-leaf for decorative purposes is of great antiquity, and although its first use as a bookbinding decoration is not clearly established it has certainly not been used for much more than three hundred years.

The technique of making gold-leaf, although not immediately relevant to a study of bookbinding methods, is of such unusual interest that a word should be spared to outline a craft that was first described by the elder Pliny.

The gold used is not pure gold as this is too soft for commercial use, but a 23½-carat alloy made by the addition of copper and silver. The initial small ingot is rolled into a ribbon 120 feet long and one-thousandth of an inch thick. The ribbon is then sandwiched between small sheets of vellum, and the resulting "cutch" is hammered so that the piece of ribbon is extended into a sheet which is divided again into small pieces and interleaved into a "shodder" consisting of eight hundred gold-beater's skins made from the intestine of an ox. The "shodder" is hammered until the gold is ready for transfer to an interleaved "mould" which consists of extremely thin gold-beater's skin, but before being placed in the "mould" the surface of the gold-leaf is cleaned with brine, a preparation which is lightly applied with the hind foot of a hare. The final hammering gives us a sheet of gold-leaf some three-millionths of an inch thick, and this is packed in between the interleaved paper sheets of a small book for dispatch to the bookbinder.

For hand lettering or tooling gold-leaf in either sheet or reel is supreme, but there is also manufactured a gold tape or reel which consists of gold-leaf carried on a transparent plastic tape, which is made by plating the ribbon electrically in a vacuum chamber. This gold tape gives eminently satisfactory results in a blocking press and is used commercially for the making of superior edition bindings.

A new metal foil called palladium is now being marketed and used on fine bindings to produce a silver finish. This foil is coated with palladium alloy, which behaves in much the same way as gold in that it retains a glow and freedom from tarnish. There are also a number of metallic and coloured stamping foils available as finishing media, and great advances have been made in the past few years towards the production of a clear, stable colour which would not deteriorate when subjected to dampness and normal wear. The majority of these colours are produced in roll or sheet form and are considerably cheaper than gold. Certainly their use by the commercial binders has increased considerably, and they are used by the edition binders when the work calls for depth and lasting qualities not found in the special case-printing inks.

TAPES AND CORDS

Tapes are made from either unbleached linen or cotton. In both cases the finished product is closely woven, has very little stretch and is manufactured in rolls varying in width from ⅜ to 2 inches. The use of tapes in publisher's casing is infrequent; where they are used they are usually ⅜-inch cotton. The commercial library binderies are increasingly sewing direct on to mull or linen spine reinforcement, and where tapes are used for conventional binding they are normally cotton tapes, but for all sizeable work which is usually hand sewn and for all high-class bindings unbleached stiffened linen tapes are used.

Cords are today used by the hand binders, and the cords used by these craftsmen are made of unsized hemp with a good long fibre so that the ends or slips can be frayed out, but occasionally for fine work an Italian linen is used.

Mull plays an important part in contemporary binding and casing as it often serves to reinforce the glued-up spine and also reinforces the joint in place of or in addition to tapes. It consists of an open-weave cotton fabric, and there is now a special type of mull being marketed with bands of heavier threads running across the mull at intervals of two inches or so, and these re-inforced strips are designed to give extra strength to the hinge and replace tapes.

A new material with which a number of edition binders are experimenting in place of mull is a bonded fibre fabric. This is a man-made fabric from cellulose waste which is both cheap to produce and made in a variety of strengths and thicknesses.

BOARDS

Three types of boards are now used in bookmaking and book-binding, and they are: (i) strawboard; (ii) millboard; and (iii) greyboard.

(i) *Strawboard* is a cheap yellowish board made largely from straw and produced in Holland. It is not particularly tough, and a sharp knock at a corner will result in a permanent loss of shape, but it is nevertheless the most widely used board for both casing and library binding. The thickness of these boards is calculated by the weight of a single board, which usually measures 30×25 inches. The weight used varies from $\frac{1}{2}$ to 4 pounds, and the average crown octavo library binding would, for example, carry a $1\frac{1}{2}$–2-pound board.

(ii) *Millboard* is made in its finest grades from old hemp rope, and the finished dark boards are highly calendered to make an extremely tough and hard-wearing material which is only used

45

today in the few distinguished craft binderies left to carry on the tradition.

The more usual millboard is also dark grey and is manufactured from a wide variety of materials which all have in common the fact that they produce a long, tough fibre—sacking, rope, waste hemp and high-grade paper.

(iii) *Greyboard* represents an intermediate stage between strawboard and millboard. It is a fairly compact, hard-wearing board which is easily worked, and together with an inferior type of *greyboard*, known as *chipboard*, it came into favour because the supply of Dutch strawboard was erratic. It is marketed in two ways, either by the number of boards to a hundredweight—6os means sixty boards measuring 40 × 30 inches—or by thickness—0·050 inch, this latter being approximately equivalent in thickness to 1 pound strawboard.

CHAPTER FIVE

Bookbinding by hand—forwarding.
Part One

THE DIVISION of labour in a craft bindery is usually between the women and girls who collate, pull down, repair and sew; the forwarders who carry out the processes from sewing right through to and including casing, and the finisher who is responsible for the lettering, decoration and final appearance of the bound book. Today the term forwarding is more often used to include all processes prior to finishing, but the old use of the term is still retained in referring to a forwarder who is a fully qualified book-binder specializing in the intermediate stages which lie between the point where the book is sewn and where it is ready to be lettered.

In the binding of a book there are infinite variations in the refinements of the techniques, but the general pattern of processes which are followed in binding a book by hand is fairly consistent. It must, however, be recognized that the technique is modified by the craftsman working in the library bindery, and his colleague working in the commercial library bindery modifies it even more substantially. Nevertheless giving a book a "flexible" binding or binding it in "boards extra" remain the basic book bindery tech-niques. A bookbinder trained to carry out such binding will be able to do his work more effectively and more efficiently even though he be engaged in an edition binders on a blocking press, and certainly a librarian who understands the basic methods of bookbinding will be able not only to appreciate and care for the older books in his library, but will also learn a good deal of the basic pattern that has influenced all classes of bookmaking today.

The first step is to make sure that the book is in fact worth binding by checking that it is complete, and the girls who carry out these preliminary processes first collate all the books to ensure that they are not imperfect. Frontispiece, title-page, preliminaries and illustrations are all checked and then the text is examined by fanning the leaves and counting the contents of each signature, which are then checked again to see that they follow each other correctly and are all complete. It is obviously a simple but quite important operation.

The next stage is known as "pulling" or "pulling down", and consists of removing the old covers and separating the sections. If the book has previously been bound the boards will be laced on with slips or lacing cords, and these must be cut away and the leather pulled from the spine. The residue of leather and glue is carefully scraped away from the spine without damaging the sections. The hollow bound book presents less of a problem, and the back hollow is split and pulled away, leaving a lining to be scraped off the spine. The cased book is merely split down the inner joints and pulled away, or, if the casing allows, the whole of both the case and the lining are stripped off with one firm pull.

The separation of the sections is achieved by carefully cutting away the sewing at the centre of each section and lifting the freed section clear then cleaning off any surplus glue. Old glue is occasionally rather intractable, and it is then soaked with paste and removed after it has been softened, but for an expensive book this is a dangerous operation as it can easily result in glue stains at the inner margins. The book has been reduced to a series of sections once again, but before the work of reassembling can start it is necessary for the old backing creases to be removed. These creases which are more strongly marked at the beginning and end of the book have been put there during the initial making in order to provide a protecting and retaining ridge for the boards, and also to enable the book to keep its shape and finally to ensure that the pages turn easily. They must be removed as the sections cannot be repaired, sewn and trimmed satisfactorily if they retain the old creases. The method is quite simple as the sections are placed two or three at a time between binder's boards on a block or on the knocking-down iron fitted into a lying press, and are then hammered with a clean, broad-faced hammer. Older books can more satisfactorily be given their original shape by gently bending the spine edge of each section with the fingers.

The spine of the book is checked to ensure that it is absolutely free from old glue, and the book is then passed on to be repaired. The repairing of a book covers dry cleaning, washing, re-sizing, removing stains, guarding, mounting and mending. Most of these processes are dealt with in the chapter on the care and repair of books, but guarding is an essential part of the re-binding of any book, and it will accordingly be described at this point.

The amount of guarding is related to the care taken in pulling down a book and the bulkiness of the paper used for printing the book. An excessive amount of guarding will produce a spine which is so swollen that if it is nipped sufficiently to allow it to be adequately rounded, there is a risk of squashing the threads through the paper. If necessary, it is advisable, particularly with thin paper, to leave pages that are slightly torn at the spine rather than bulk up the spine excessively. It is usual to guard the first and last pairs of pages in each section as these are subjected to the greatest strain and can serve, if necessary, to hold the remaining pairs of leaves fairly tightly in position. The material used to make these guards varies considerably, ranging from linen for the first and last sections to fine tissue strips. Cockerell recommends Whatman's Banknote paper for the work, but a good Bank paper would seem to be generally adequate. The paper is reduced to half-inch strips, and these can be pasted quite easily if a few are piled on a stone slab and then picked off as they are required. The use of gummed reinforcing rolls of tissue for this work is a commercial binding practice which has now been accepted by many craft binders. Plates and maps require special treatment, and the usual practice is to provide plates consisting of individual leaves with a guard which folds round the section and can be stitched with it. Pairs of illustrations are guarded in the usual way, and a book which consists entirely of single leaves is made up into pairs of leaves by guarding and then sewing through the guard or by binding the book by the unsewn process.

Folded maps or illustrations are usually mounted on linen in order to ensure that the map or illustration is given a life commensurate with the life of the book. The guard provided is usually slightly wider than page size so that the map or illustration can be "thrown out", and the overlap of the guard is then carried round the appropriate section, preferably at the end of the book, and then sewn in.

The greatest strain and wear on any book is at the inner joints, and as the strength of inner joints is partly dependent on the end-papers a good deal of ingenuity has been displayed in devising various methods of joining and folding sheets of paper together so that they give both strength and flexibility.

In the publisher's case the endpaper usually consists of a simple fold of text paper tipped on to the first and last sections, and it is true to say that the inner joints and therefore the whole construction of the book are just as strong as this tipped leaf is effective. In commercial library binding various endpapers are used, but the most usual consists of a pair of leaves made out of strong, heavy-weight paper reinforced with a linen strip and then caught up in the sewing.

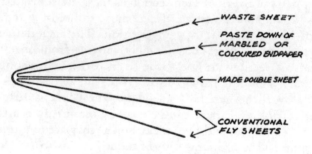

THE MADE ENDPAPER

In hand binding, the most popular endpaper is known as the "made" end, and it is incorporated in the binding by either sewing or tipping. The blank side of half a piece of coloured or marbled paper is pasted to a piece of white paper of the same size, and after nipping and drying this double sheet is edged into another fold of white paper. The endpaper is then tipped into the book with a $\frac{3}{16}$-inch margin of paste and sewn through.

The so-called provincial made endpaper has a modification which is designed to overcome the tendency of the "made" paper to pull at the sections, but the best known of these more elaborate endpaper foldings is a type of accordion pleating popularized by

Douglas Cockerell and known as the zig-zag endpaper. Although as with most craft processes a description of the method used for making such endpapers makes it appear most elaborate and

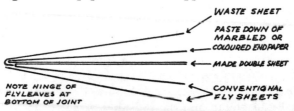

THE PROVINCIAL MADE ENDPAPER

complex, an experiment with folded paper will make it a good deal clearer.

An over-large folded sheet of paper A is given a strip of paste at X, and a "made" fold of endpaper B is fastened to A at X, giving A a pleated fold. A further pair of leaves C is inserted between the lower pair of leaves separating B from A, and then the endpaper is completed by cutting away the upper leaf of A as waste, pasting down the upper leaf of B and sewing through the fold to give it a firm but expanding link with the book.

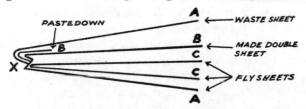

THE ZIG-ZAG ENDPAPER

It is certainly a strong and effective endpaper, but occasionally critics, including Bernard C. Middleton, have suggested that although quite suitable for leather it is otherwise a rather time-consuming and bulky endpaper. Variations are endless, and readers who wish to pursue the matter further are recommended to read the books and periodicals referred to at the end of this book.

To give the books solidity and to sharpen the folds the sections are next subjected to a "beating", a rather slow, cumbersome and unnecessarily elaborate method whereby the sections are hammered down a few at a time on a flat stone or iron. Most bookbinders today are satisfied with the standing iron press which applies sufficient pressure to produce the necessary shape, but can, of course, if used carelessly deaden the print and so spoil the appearance of the hand-printed page.

The book may now be ready to be trimmed if it has been sewn on cords, or it may be trimmed at a later stage after the boards have been added. It is a matter of choice, depending on the type of book being bound and the finishing that is proposed for the book. Cutting the book in boards gives the edges a smoothness and a finish that is functionally sound and often aesthetically appropriate, but the rough gilt appearance of the book which is gilded before sewing has a freedom from the harshness of the solid smooth gilt which makes it particularly attractive for slim books printed in the larger founts on hand-made paper. The majority of books bound in the craft bindery are trimmed in boards, and it will be at that point that trimming, edge-gilding and edge-colouring will be dealt with.

The marking up of the spine of the book is carried out so that the sewer can have a clear indication of the position of the tapes or cords and the kettle stitch. The usual practice is to give a book five bands which divides the spine into six rectangles with the rectangle at the tail slightly larger than the remaining five equal rectangles. The conventional practice is to saw across the back so that the cords and kettle stitch will fit into the recesses, but there seems to be general agreement that this practice is quite undesirable as it weakens the binding and is usually followed in any event by the fitting of false bands.

The book is now ready for sewing, and the sewing frame is set up. This simple piece of binding equipment is a direct link with early bookbinding as the design has changed very little over the centuries. It consists of a horizontal slotted wooden platform out of which rise two threaded wooden uprights supporting a movable cross-bar. The strings or cords on to which the book is to be sewn are tied between the base, where they are fixed with metal keys, and the cross-bar to which they are attached by means of a series of cord loops. The strings or cords are adjustable to coincide with the markings and then tightened up ready for the actual sewing to begin.

The first section is laid on the platform of the sewing frame so that the back of the section presses against the cords, which must coincide with the markings. The needle carrying the linen thread is inserted at the point where the position of the kettle stitch at the head of the book is marked and sewn in, and the thread is then passed into the centre of the fold, and out, and then around the first cord and back into the fold. The thread is carried in and out of the section, passing round each cord until the point of the tail kettle stitch is reached and the needle carries the thread out ready for the next section. The second section is sewn in similar fashion, but when the thread comes out at the head kettle stitch mark it is tied to the loose end at the beginning of the first section. The third and all subsequent sections are dealt with in much the same way, but when the thread passes out at the end of the section it is threaded back to link it to the previous sections with a kettle stitch. The final section is reinforced with a double kettle stitch in order to lock the thread.

As the sewing proceeds it is necessary to ensure that an even tension is maintained both in the actual sewing and in the making of kettle stitches, and to facilitate this the sections are lightly knocked down with a loaded stick. This flexible method of sewing relies on the use of one continuous linen thread running through the whole of the sewing of the book, and when one length of the thread is used up it is joined to another by means of an interlocking slip knot known as a weaver's knot, and this knot is made so that it lies inside the section.

If several books of the same size are being sewn on to sunken cords or tapes at the same time it is the practice to sew them in one continuous operation to the same cords, but inevitably each separate book requires a separate thread. When the sewing is complete the cords are released and a sufficient margin of cord is pulled through to allow each book the necessary overlap to make the slips before they are separated and cut apart.

In contrast to this method of sewing individual sections, known as sewing "all-along", is the method of sewing known as "sewing two on". In this process the first and last sections are usually sewn

53

all along, but intermediate sections are sewn to the cords or tapes in pairs, the thread passing after each complete stitch to the adjoining section so that the amount of sewing per section is reduced by half, and this results in a lessening of the swelling at the spine. The disadvantage is an obvious reduction in strength, but with a book consisting of a large number of very thin sections it reduces the swelling to manageable proportions.

Overcasting is rarely used in extra binding, but it is a method of hand sewing fairly widely used in library binderies and consists of sewing together the first two sections of the book by passing the thread through the two sections and back across the back of the sections. The third and subsequent sections are laid on the frame and sewn to the second or adjoining section so that each section is firmly sewn to the adjoining section, and the finished sewing gives a strong book which tends to be rather unsatisfactory for normal use because of the restriction of the spine, but when the margin is adequate and the paper thin it has something to recommend it. With weak or brittle paper that cannot be treated satisfactorily by the "unsewn" method there is a great deal to be said in its favour, particularly if in such cases the section is sewn to the two sections below it.

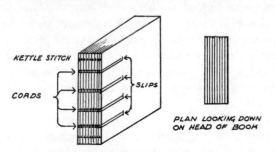

KETTLE STITCH

CORDS

SLIPS

PLAN LOOKING DOWN ON HEAD OF BOOK

THE BOOK AFTER SEWING

After the book has been sewn the cords are cut so as to leave an inch and a half or so overlapping, and these overlapping pieces of cord are known as "slips". The slips are subsequently frayed out so that after they have been laced on to the boards they lie flat and do not leave a projecting ridge through the covering material.

The book is then knocked up so that all the pages are level, and it is then ready for gluing up and subsequently for rounding and backing. The thin flexible glue is applied working outwards from the centre of the spine and is well brushed in so that it penetrates between the sections. When the glue has ceased to be tacky the book can be rounded. The purpose of rounding has already been discussed in Chapter One, and in hand binding it is particularly necessary to obtain a well-rounded but not exaggerated curve on the spine so that the covering of the spine is smooth and can be easily lettered, and also so that the book will keep its shape and open easily. All these advantages are achieved by hammering the spine in such a way that it is made slightly convex. The book is laid on a flat solid surface, and with the left hand holding the book and forcing the sections forward at the spine by pressure at the fore-edge, the spine is given a gentle hammering to hold the book in the partly rounded shape imparted by the left hand. The book is then turned over and both the pressure and the hammering repeated so that a round of about one-third of a circle is given to the book. A book that is given an exaggerated roundness does not look well and is difficult to open. On the other hand, an inadequately rounded book will not only be difficult to back but will subsequently tend to start and revert to a flat-back after use.

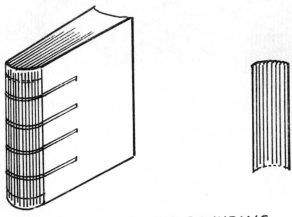

THE BOOK AFTER ROUNDING

The backing of a hand-bound book is a simple process that demands a gentle hand and a nice judgement. The aim is to hammer over the rounded spine so that it provides a step against which the boards of the book can lie and enable the book to open more easily, but it also serves to lock the sections together, and this helps the book to keep its shape. For the majority of books the process consists of fastening the book in a backing press in such a way that the front and back of the book project a little above the iron edges of the press. The spine is then gently hammered, working out from the centre so that it is finally bent over the edges of the backing press. With books sewn on tapes or sawn in cords this presents little difficulty, but it is a task of some complexity with a spine bearing raised cords as a small hammer has to be used between the cords, and great care is necessary to avoid damaging the sewing.

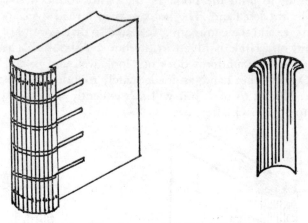

THE BOOK AFTER BACKING

A fairly detailed consideration of the various types of board used in bookbinding is given in the chapter on the materials of bookbinding, but in hand bookbinding we are only concerned with millboard. This dark grey board is extremely hard and strong and as a consequence gives a permanent solidity and sharpness to the finished binding. The tendency in this class of binding is to give a book an extra heavy board, but it is an undesirable practice

REINFORCING THE PAGES

1. LIBRARY BINDERY. Reinforcing by hand

2. COMMERCIAL BINDERY. Reinforcing by machine and hand

3.
LIBRARY BINDERY.
Sewing by hand on
a sewing frame

4.
COMMERCIAL BINDERY.
Sewing by machine using
a Martini sewing on three
tapes

5. LIBRARY BINDERY. The single-edge guillotine trimming the tail

6. COMMERCIAL BINDERY. The three-edge guillotine trimming
head and tail simultaneously

7.   LIBRARY BINDERY. Hand rounding and backing. *The process is nearly finished and the ridge produced by the backing is clearly shown*

ROUNDING AND BACKING

8. COMMERCIAL BINDERY. Automatic rounding and backing. *The processed books can be seen in the foreground*

9. COMMERCIAL BINDERY. A detail of the automatic rounding and backing machine showing the two jaws holding the book ready for the concave roller

10. **LIBRARY BINDERY.** Lacing on the boards

11. **COMMERCIAL BINDERY.** The case-making machine. *The glue roller is on the left, the boards on the right. A pair of boards can be seen moving to meet the piece of glued cloth and the case will subsequently be carried out on the conveyor belt in the foreground*

12. LIBRARY BINDERY. Lettering by hand using a pallet. *In the right foreground may be seen a frame of type. Two individual letter tools may be seen in the left foreground*

13. COMMERCIAL BINDERY. Lettering by machine. *The various metal slugs may be seen on the left and these are produced by the operator using the keyboard on the right*

14. COMMERCIAL BINDERY. Lettering by machine. *The blocking press is backed with a slug which is heated and then brought into contact with the roll of foil and the case*

for a book which is likely to be submitted to any considerable amount of use as it throws an unnecessary strain on the general construction of the binding. A practice which was once widely advocated for many classes of books and their binding is the use of split boards, and these are occasionally made by actually slitting the board along its length with a sharp knife, but the more usual practice is to glue or paste together a thick and thin millboard of the same size, leaving an unglued margin some two to three inches wide along the length. These boards are of a size sufficient to allow them to project beyond and protect the edges of the book, and this projection or square, as it is called, must be consistent with the weight of the board, the size of the book and the type of binding used. Allowance must also be made for the French joint if one is being used, and the final result should give us a square of something approaching one-eighth of an inch at head and tail, and three-sixteenths of an inch at the fore-edge for a well-built octavo.

It is essential that the boards should be fastened to the book so that they open easily and lie flat, and they must also be joined in such a way that the join is not visible in the finished work and yet is of sufficient strength. With cords and single boards the practice is to lay the boards in place and mark the points where the cords lie. The board is then removed and at the point marked one hole is punched with an awl from the outside about half an inch from the inner edge, and then a second hole about three-quarters of an inch from the inner edge is punched. A groove just deep enough to hold the cord is then cut leading from the edge to the first hole so that the cord will lie flush and not show through the cover on completion. Occasionally the grooves are not cut or are deliberately left shallow so that the impression of the cord will show through and give a clear indication of hand craftsmanship and possibly provide a motif for the finishing. The cords are pasted, threaded through the first hole from the outside and brought up through the second hole and trimmed off. The cords are then hammered flat and the holes closed by the same process.

Books that are hand sewn on tapes are usually given split boards, and the tapes are inserted into the split, which is glued and dried under pressure.

CHAPTER SIX

Bookbinding by hand—forwarding and finishing.
Part Two

THE PLOUGH is accepted by all authoritative textbooks as the appropriate tool for trimming the edges of the book, but it seems likely that its use is now limited to the process we have now reached, which is known as cutting in boards. In fact, this elaborate and time-consuming method is usually avoided by trimming the edges of the book with a guillotine immediately after it has been sewn, and either just before or just after the spine has been glued. Nevertheless the method of cutting in boards is the traditional method and consists of clamping the book in a heavy wooden press. One jaw of the press carries a pair of wooden guide rails within which one leg of the plough slides up and down. This leg is attached to the main leg of the plough by a wooden thread, and this leg carries a sharp chisel-like blade which is adjusted so that it just touches the book, and then by sliding the plough up and down the top of the press and gradually tightening the arms of the plough the book is cut through. With a well-shaped and sharpened plough-knife the finished edge has a smoothness and a gloss which are not readily obtainable with a guillotine. The trimming of the concave fore-edge calls for special consideration, and the difficulty is overcome by forcing the book back to its square shape and gripping it in a press. If the book is sewn on raised cords this presents some further difficulty, and slotted metal plates called trindles are fitted on the spine in such a way that the raised bands fit through the slots and thus allow the main body of the book to be forced into square.

The purpose of gilding or colouring the edges of a book is primarily protective as the intention is to give a smooth solid surface that will prevent dust being admitted. The majority of hand-bound books are gilded only at the top edge, giving us that abbreviation so familiar to all who study second-hand booksellers' catalogues of t.e.g. Occasionally all three edges are gilded, particularly when the book carries a rich finish, and this is known as "full gilt" or "gilt all round", or in the catalogues, a.e.g.

To gild a book it is locked firmly in a press and the edge to be treated is rubbed smooth with a steel scraper or a piece of glass and then sandpapered. The smooth surface is then given a coating of blacklead or red ochre, which acts as a filler and this is followed by a coating of glair made from egg albumen. The gold-leaf is then cut to the appropriate size and floated on to the prepared edge, and as the glair dries, it binds the gold-leaf to the edge of the book. When the glair has dried, the gold is burnished by rubbing through a sheet of paper with either an agate or bloodstone across the leaves. The edge is then slightly waxed and burnished direct.

Two variants on the conventional edge gilding are fore-edge painting and gauffering. Neither of them is used to any extent today, but they have a certain appeal and their production is relatively simple. The fore-edge painting is made after the fore-edge has been scraped smooth in the round, and the leaves are then fanned out and the book tied in that position so that the artist may paint the picture on the extended fore-edge. The book is subsequently restored to its normal shape and gilded with the result that the fore-edge painting only becomes visible on fanning out the pages.

Gauffering is a method of edge decoration which is achieved by denting, marking and pricking the finished gilded edge with heated tools or by applying the same heated tools to an additional coat of gold. The finished work is a little over-ornate for contemporary tastes.

The edges of a book can also be coloured or marbled, and very occasionally they are coloured or marbled and then gilded. The colouring consists of any conventional stain or water-colour applied quickly to the edges when they are under pressure and sealed with a little bees-wax. The process of marbling is now rarely used in modern craft bookbinding, but commercial stationery binders now use transfer paper for marbling. The paper and the technique are similar to those used by schoolboys

59

for their transfers. Mention should, however, be made of the beautifully designed marbled papers produced by Douglas Cockerell in England and by Rosamond B. Loring in the U.S.A.

In machine-made books headbands serve a simple decorative function and are made by machine and then glued to the head and tail of the spine. When headbands are used in craft binding they are hand made by passing a needle threaded with two or three differently coloured silks through the fold of the first section and then looped round a cord or vellum strip. The process is continued by passing the needle through the fold of occasional sections and twisting the silk round the cord or vellum strip until it becomes a gaily covered band of silk threads fastened securely into the book, and so providing a little additional strength where it is needed but adding a pleasantly decorative touch to the book.

Jobbing binders and the commercial binder producing the elegant edition buy their highly coloured headbands by the yard, and they are then glued on to the spine, where they serve a decorative but otherwise useless purpose.

The lining up of the spine of a book is carried out in a wide variety of ways, but they all have in common the object of producing a smooth surface so that the finishing on the spine of the finished work can be effectively carried out. The most marked irregularities on the surface of the spine are filled in with a mixture made from millboard filings and paste. The first lining of a medium soft kraft paper is then glued over the spine, covering it exactly and then rubbed down with fine sandpaper. A further layer of paper is then glued on until a smooth and slightly resilient surface is achieved. In pursuit of a really smooth surface the extra binder may build up a lining which seriously impedes the easy opening of the book, and French craft binders tend to line the spine up with many pieces of skiver which inevitably produces a stiff back.

Because the tight back bends with the spine of the book, there is a tendency for the tooling on the spine to crack after the book has been opened repeatedly and for this reason many hand-bound books are today given hollow backs. The hollow back consists of a paper tube which is the width of the spine, and one side of this tube is glued to the spine which has either been sewn on to sawn-in cords or on to tapes. Any number of these tubes can be used, and the tube is made on the spine after a preliminary lining up. The most usual method is to glue on to the spine a piece of kraft or fairly heavy wrapping-paper which is slightly longer than the spine and three times the width of the spine. The two surplus widths are glued to each other to give a tube of paper with one thickness fastened and two thicknesses free from the spine but stuck to each other. There are many variants, this particular English variety being known as "one on two off". The surplus at the head and tail is trimmed off.

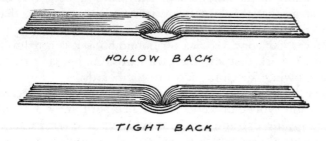

HOLLOW BACK

TIGHT BACK

Leather may be used to cover the whole of the book, in which case it is occasionally said to be "whole-bound". It may possibly be used to cover the back and one-third of the width of the boards. The corners are also covered with leather to the same depth measured diagonally as the overlap from the back of the book, and such a binding is known as "three-quarter-bound". The more usual style is known as "half-bound" and consists of a leather back piece which extends one-fifth of the way across the boards and carries corners in proportion. The remainder of the binding in such cases is usually covered with a carefully chosen cloth.

In the whole-bound book it is usual to prepare a paper pattern of the piece of leather required in order to ensure that this extremely expensive material is not spoilt or poorly fitting. The pattern made is then carefully fitted on to the selected skin, and for extra binding only the back and sides of the skin are used, with the spine of the skin running along the spine of the book. In the finest class of binding it is the practice to use the smaller skins for the smaller books so that the thickness of the leather is appropriate and paring is reduced to a minimum.

The trimming down or paring of skins is carried out so that the turn-in will not project unduly inside the boards, and on occasions paring is used on the part of the skin which covers the back and the joints so that the book will subsequently open easily and the leather will fit snugly to the raised cords.

Paste is used to soften the leather and provide a slow-setting adhesive which will allow the leather to be worked easily and permit such operations as working the leather round the bands and the fixing of the raised bands with band nippers. It is usually at this stage that the corners are trimmed or mitred so that the fold over inside the board is not too bulky.

With the half- or three-quarter-bound book it is usual to finish the leather work first and then trim any roughness at the edges before applying the cloth pieces to the boards.

When the book has been fully covered and has been carefully checked and rubbed down to ensure a smooth finish, it is tied up until it is quite dry and set. This tying up is carried out with a linen sewing thread which is tied round the joint at the back of the book in order to ensure a nicely defined shape.

The lettering, decoration and the final treatment of the bound book is known as finishing. The lettering and decoration can be carried out either by blind tooling or gold tooling. Blind tooling is the impression made by a finishing tool without using gold-leaf, foil, or any other material as a medium.

Inevitably the finisher is mostly concerned with lettering the titles and authors of books. The most usual method is by the application of heated bookbinder's type set up in a pallet. This type, unlike printer's type, is extremely hard-wearing and is made of brass. It is set up in point sizes similar to conventional type and is composed from a frame by the finisher or his apprentice, who assembles it in a stick, usually consisting of only one line of type. This stick or pallet is equipped with a wooden handle, and the assembled type is fastened in and then heated. Unfortunately this type is costly to buy and expensive to produce and the smallness of demand restricts the range and beauty of the faces available. The larger sizes of type are made on separate hand tools so that each letter requires a separate impression—an operation calling for a good eye and a high degree of skill.

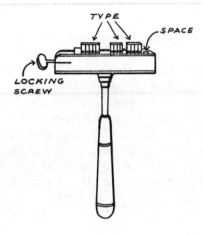

PALLET OR
TYPEHOLDER

The relative sizes and arrangement of lettering vary considerably. In the majority of hand-bound books it is the practice to letter the title in the second panel from the head, followed by the author's name in the third or fourth panel and the volume number in the fourth panel, but the placing varies with the individual customer and the individual design. A well-lettered volume usually carries the single lines of type slightly above the centre of the panel and achieves a nice appearance by alternating long and short lines. Certainly well-justified lines of type look surprisingly ugly.

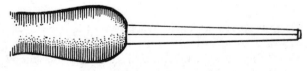

A HAND LETTER

The decoration on the back of the book can vary considerably. The simplest and one of the most attractive designs is that which uses a gold line round each panel with the corners neatly mitred. The full-gilt decoration implies that each panel, including those carrying lettering, is given a mitred line and that those panels carrying no lettering are decorated. The decoration can consist of a simple repetitive piece in the centre of the panel, but more usually consists of a carefully composed design of arabesques.

It is often the practice to tool the sides of the book if it is fully bound and fully gilt. It is possible in the limited space of the sides of a book to produce the most ingenious, elaborate and tiresome decoration, and although it would be foolish to dogmatize in matters of taste, there can surely be little doubt that many books have been bound with a high degree of skill and craftsmanship, only to be spoilt by an over-elaborate and tasteless design. The aim should be to produce an original and attractive contemporary design which fits the subject of the book bound and is free from the decorative conventions of fifty years ago.

A ROLL

The design is carried out with a set of simple tools. All of these finishing tools are individual hand tools, and the most frequently used is the "fillet" or "roll", which consists of a metal wheel carrying a line or lines or occasionally carrying a simple repetitive design such as a chain of flowers in relief on the edge. The wheel

64

is supported through its axis by a rod which ends in a wooden handle, and the heated fillet is used to produce a straight line or a line consisting of a repeated design. There are in addition gouges which are used for producing curved lines. The non-continuous straight line such as that used across the backs of books to separate title from author is produced with a finishing tool called rather confusingly a pallet, and this consists of a strongly made piece of heavy tapered metal. Finally there are the individual tools consisting of simple pictorial designs such as symmetrical flowers, or dots, or stars or any small outline in relief which can be used either to reinforce or to build up a design.

The actual technique of finishing involves the preparation of the leather, the preparation of the design, the actual tooling and variations in the technique of decoration.

It is the practice to smooth grained leather such as morocco with a heated polishing iron which is worked across the leather sufficiently to give a smooth working surface. The leather is then treated to make the surface ready to receive the heated tools by washing it. The first wash may consist of water with a little added glycerine if the leather appears to be dry; on the other hand, acid-free vinegar may be used to remove the surface grease. A paste wash may then follow in order to fill the pores of the skin and give a smooth finish, but occasionally the book is given a slightly milky appearance as a result of a heavy paste wash, and some binders prefer a gelatine wash as a filler.

The tooling can now be carried out either blind or in gold. Blind tooling gives an impression and a design by darkening and denting the leather with a hot tool which is usually in intaglio so that the finished work stands up in relief. It can be used quite effectively in combination with finishing in gold.

Before gold-leaf can be applied to a book it needs a medium to hold it, and this medium must be responsive to heat so that when the heat is applied it will dry out and draw the gold-leaf down on to the leather and so produce a permanent gold finish. The material used to produce this result is called glair, which is invariably made from an albumen base and usually consists of a mixture of white of egg and vinegar.

The finisher then lays out his design which he may do directly

65

on the leather with the point of a folder if it is simple enough but but it is more usual to work out the design in final detail on a paper pattern which is folded over the covers, and the tools are then applied directly to the paper, giving a blind impression on the leather. Occasionally the extra binder may work out his design in full on a scrap piece of leather. In any event the leather is then lightly brushed with Vaseline and the gold-leaf is applied as required with a little pressure so that the design in relief shows through. This gold-leaf is taken from the interleaved book of gold and laid on a leather cushion, where it is cut into appropriately sized pieces with a soft-edged pallet knife, and then picked up from the cushion by a pad of very slightly greased cotton wool. It is possible to apply the gold by means of a plastic tape which carries it until the heat is applied through it, but it seems fairly certain that such a medium takes away something of the sharpness of the impression.

The lettering is carried out through the gold by means of impressing hot brass type assembled in a hand pallet. The heat is applied to the type by means of a simply constructed small hot metal plate heated by gas or electricity, and the loaded pallet is laid on this plate. The heat used varies with type, colouring and age of the leather, but it is usually just hot enough to hiss if dampened. The line of type is impressed across the back of the book with a firm even pressure so that the type is nicely impressed in such a way that it is well balanced on either back or cover.

The various finishing tools are heated and applied through the gold, and when the book is completely lettered and decorated the surplus gold is rubbed off with a soft rubber or a gold rag, which is subsequently returned to the manufacturer of the gold-leaf so that the gold may be reclaimed.

Finishing in blind merely lacks the gold medium, but the strength and depth of letter and line can be increased by softening the leather with water and then applying the tools at such a heat that they darken the leather without damaging it. This particular variation is known as antique tooling, but in spite of that it is much used in contemporary binding, particularly French hand binding.

The finisher occasionally enamels in a series of blind lines and so produces an intaglio design in contrasting colours, but it is a process that is usually reserved for a simple contrasting rule. A more subtle and difficult operation is that of inlaying, a process that could usually be more accurately called onlaying as it consists of pasting on to the leather of the cover a finely pared piece of leather of a different colour which has been cut to fit the design already tooled on the cover. Only very occasionally is a design inlaid, and this is carried out by cutting out the leather from the design that has been blinded in and then fitting in and pasting down a carefully shaped piece of contrasting leather. Both techniques are finished by smoothing off the edge of the inlay by tooling either in gold or blind.

It would be a convenience from the student's point of view if the processes of hand bookbinding fell quite clearly and conveniently into the three stages of preparation, forwarding and finishing, but unfortunately and most confusingly the majority of hand bookbinders carry out a forwarding process after the finishing of the book in that they paste down the end sheets and give the book a final pressing. The process is fairly straightforward, but of considerable importance in that the durability of the binding hinges on this operation. It is carried out by opening the book and laying the cover on to a raised block, after which the surplus endpapers or waste sheets are removed and the endpaper selected as a paste down is carefully pressed into the hinge and marked off so that it fits neatly over the overlapping leather inside the cover. It is then cut to size, pasted and fitted carefully so that it adheres into the joint and lies exactly on the inside cover.

All that remains is for the printed book to be pressed, and checked and opened. The method of opening is one that should be known and carried out by librarians on all books that are of any considerable value and are being opened for the first time, either as new or after rebinding. It is designed to ensure that the book will subsequently open evenly and not fall open at the one place as a result of having been carelessly forced open. A book that has been so maltreated is said to have had its back broken—a pardonable exaggeration because although in fact the spine is only heavily creased it will inevitably result in such a strain in the structure that the binding will inevitably break down at that

67

point. A craft binder opens a newly bound book by opening each board in turn, and as he does so he presses the board gently into the joint. The book is then opened a few pages at a time at the front and back alternately, and the opened pages gently pressed down so that when the process is finished a well-bound book will, when opened, come to rest with the pages lying open in a fairly symmetrical fan-shaped pattern.

CHAPTER SEVEN

The making of a book.
The process of casing or edition binding

IT WOULD be interesting but not directly relevant to consider in some detail the various methods of printing a book, but it is necessary for our purpose to know something of the physical make-up of a book; to know how a book is made and why it is made in that particular way if we are to understand and appreciate the final processes used in producing a new book and in subsequently re-binding that book.

When a book is printed it is the practice to set up and print as many pages in one operation as can be managed efficiently and economically. It is not unusual for sixty-four pages to be produced on a machine printing quad crown (30 × 40 inches), and there are many machines in use printing on eight crown sheets (40 × 60 inches), giving us one hundred and twenty-eight pages on the two sides of one sheet.

The cutting and folding of these sheets is carried out in edition work by special machines which deliver the sheets in sixteen or thirty-two page sections. The method of folding the sheets varies with the individual machines, and as each machine will only fold in one particular way it follows that the imposition of the printed page must be related to the type of folding machine which it is proposed to use. As the folded sheets come from the folder they are passed through a bundling machine, which presses the sections together into a large bundle and fastens a string or wrapper round the bundle. It is a relatively small machine in most factories and can be moved from machine to machine, but it is quite indispensable if the sewing is not being carried out immediately after folding. Its advantages are that it makes the sections more compact and easier to handle as without such bundling sections tend to curl. It has the additional advantage of reducing the possibility of mixed sections.

In some factories the endpapers are fastened at this stage to the first and last sections by applying a thin strip of adhesive to the inner or spine edge of the section, and the endpaper is then pressed down, giving a tipped endpaper, as this particular method of fastening an individual page or pair of pages is called. It is, of course, widely used for individual plates in the text which are given a narrow strip of paste and fastened into the fold of the appropriate section. The process is only used where it is necessary for the illustration to coincide with the text. Publishers are showing an increased awareness of the fact that this technique weakens the finished book, and the tendency is now to print the plates in pairs and then to fold this pair of leaves round the section so that it becomes an integral part of the book. A less frequently used method but one that is growing in popularity is to assemble the plates at the end of the text. Occasionally the plates are printed with a surplus at the inner edge so that the stub folds round the section, and is then sewn in as part of the book.

The printed sections of the book are known as signatures, a term which is likely to cause some confusion as it is also used to indicate the small letter or figure which usually appears at the foot of the front page of each section so that it can be readily distinguished. When the signatures have been unpacked from the bundles—each bundle inevitably contains only the one section—they are piled in compartments arranged in a long table and the process of assembling the sections, known as "gathering" is then carried out by a girl walking the length of the table and picking up a section or signature from each compartment. An alternative method is that whereby a number of girls sit round a slowly revolving table and pick up a section from each of the compartments round the circumference.

There is, of course, a gathering machine which is a comparatively recent invention and which works quite successfully in the larger factories. This machine consists of a conveyor belt carrying round a number of compartments, each containing copies of one section. A series of arms pick up the sections as they move along the machine and they transfer the sections in correct order to a corresponding series of raised and tilted boxes on the other side of the machine. An average machine will have twenty stations operating at the same time, and a simple trip mechanism stops the machine in the event of a faulty pick-up and operates a flag at the particular box where the mechanism has failed.

If gathering machines worked perfectly, there would be no need for the assembled sections to be checked or collated. The process of examining the book to ensure that it is complete is often carried out by a simple visual check of the collating marks, which are specially printed on the spine edge of the outer pair of leaves of each section, starting at the top for the first section and dropping a little with each successive section so that in the correctly assembled book the collation marks appear as a heavy diagonal line running across the spine. The alternative method is by checking the actual signatures appearing at the bottom of the first page of each section.

Endpapers may have already been affixed, but the more usual practice is to carry out the process at this stage. The paper used and the number of pages in endpapers may vary considerably, but the endpaper is generally made of the same paper as that of the text and in a single sheet. One leaf is then tipped to the body of that work and the other leaf pasted down on the board in due course. Care must be taken to ensure that the grain of the end-paper runs parallel to the back of the book so that any contraction across the grain is minimized and warping is checked.

It is not proposed to discuss at any length that quite unsatisfactory method of fastening a book together by wire staples. This type of fastening is of two kinds—in the first, saddle stitching, the signatures are stitched through the fold, in the second, side stitching, the staples stab through the thickness of the book, and machines can now cope with thicknesses up to $2\frac{1}{2}$ inches. It is a process that has been used intermittently for more than half a century, and the curious may find the occasional book stitched in this way during the last century and still holding together; but by and large it is an ugly and inefficient process which should be reserved for the most ephemeral of printed material.

There are a large number of different book-sewing machines on the market today, varying from the oversewing machine, which sews each section to the preceding one by passing a thread through the spine-edge of each section and bringing it out through the adjoining section, to the side sewing machine, which punches a series of holes near the book-edge, and the punch is followed by a needle which carries forward a locked loopstitch along the length of the back.

The British book trade and library bookbinders confine themselves almost entirely to two or three book-stitching machines, and as they are all fairly similar in the method of operation the working of only one machine will be described. This machine, the Martini, will sew books from $1\frac{1}{2}$ to 17 inches high and from $1\frac{1}{2}$ to 11 inches wide on to six tapes, using twelve stitches, each stitch being sewn with a separate thread. There is no limit to the number of sections and the thickness of the book, and given competent operators this machine can sew 8,000 to 11,000 signatures a day as compared with the hand sewer, who usually sews not more than 300 signatures a day. The machine consists of up to six reels of tape mounted at the top of the machine and supported by up to twelve spools of cotton thread, all of which are fed down into the main body of the machine to a series of specially designed spiral needles. It is the construction of this needle with its crochet-like spiral eye that distinguishes this particular machine. Each signature of the book is opened at the centre fold and then fed by hand on to a metal saddle which carries the signature forward to the stitching needles and then presses it against the tapes which in the final stages run horizontally from the centre to the back of the machine. At this point the sewing needles carrying the threads from the previous sections pass through the stabbed holes, and the thread is then picked up and transferred inside the fold to the next needle and pulled through to the outer fold, where it is carried across the tape—if tapes are being used—and given a mock kettle stitch. The needles then move upwards in preparation for the next section.

As each group of signatures is sewn together making the complete sewn text of a book the machine gives a double catch stitch to lock the sewing effectively prior to the first signature of the next book being fed on to the saddle. At the back of the machine the horizontal tray carrying the sewn books with continuous tapes linking them all is unloaded by drawing through the necessary surplus of tape for each book, and then cutting these tapes to reduce them to individual items. A similar machine has a rather interesting modification in that it incorporates a paster which enables the operator to apply a thin strip of paste to the back fold of the first and last sections and by doing so give a little extra strength to the back at two vital points.

Tapes are now only used occasionally in publishers' casing, and this would seem to be no serious loss as the practice of sewing books on tapes and then fastening the tapes down with the weakest of endpapers was never likely to produce a strong hard-wearing book. The best of the present practices is known as French sewing. This consists of sewing on to a piece of mull which is fed through the machine in a continuous roll almost the length of the book, and this mull is sewn thoroughly to the spine of the book and then given an overlap of usually about three-quarters of an inch at the back and front so as to provide a useful reinforcement to the endpaper, but the far more usual practice is to rely merely on the sewing and then to apply the mull at a later stage.

The books are taken from the sewing machine, the mull is cut, and they are then stacked carefully with back and fore-edge alternating so that they can be handled easily with their swollen spines by the operator of the nipping or smashing machine. Both these machines are designed to flatten the spines and give the book solidity. The nipper consists of a pair of loaded metal jaws which subject the spine to such considerable pressure that the spine is left only slightly thicker than the body of the book, and so leaves sufficient margin for the subsequent rounding and backing. The smasher, unlike the nipper, consists of a series of rollers fed by a conveyor belt, and the books pass under the heavy rollers, and this process inevitably flattens both spine and body to the same level.

The books are ready to be trimmed and the bookbinder's guillotine usually consists of a three-bladed cutter which trims the three edges of the book with one handling. The books are clamped down on the platform and the cutting operations then follow automatically—first the fore-edge is trimmed and this is followed by two knives cutting the head and tail simultaneously. A more complex machine has a continuous trimming operation

73

and unlike the previous machine it is not stopped after the fore-edge cut. The machine consists of a series of four clamped boxes each carrying its own cutting bed and as the boxes rotate to the four stations they are loaded, trimmed at the fore-edge, trimmed at the head and tail and then unloaded. This is a most interesting machine the usefulness of which has recently been extended by the addition of a vacuum pick-up and conveyor to carry the waste paper to a baler which compresses it for the scrap merchant.

It must be mentioned that since the last war there has been a quickening in the pace of mechanization particularly in the edition binders factory. There are not only larger and faster machines but there is also an equally inevitable trend towards continuous straight-line production so that by means of conveyor belts and automatic feeds one large machine is linked up with another.

Gluing in edition binding takes place at any one of three points in the making of a book. Many firms are now gluing up first and reducing the swelling in the spine afterwards but it seems to be agreed that such a procedure tends to produce a rather inadequately rounded and backed book. A more usual point for gluing is just before trimming as this ensures that if the books are carefully knocked up before gluing and then are processed fairly soon after trimming there is produced a well-shaped book which has not started or slid as a result of being subjected to the pressure of the guillotine clamp. The traditional point for gluing in publisher's casework, and incidentally, in other classes of binding is after trimming. If the edition is small and the work of a fairly high standard a thin flexible glue is brushed well into the spine by hand, working from the centre to the end, and in this way the glue penetrates between the curves of the folds of the sections where it can do its work properly. The majority of books are, however, glued on a fairly large gluing machine which carries the sections along with their spines facing vertically downwards and as they move along they are jogged until the edges are quite even. A revolving roller coats the backs, but unfortunately it does not usually give that degree of penetration between the signatures that even a publisher's casing should have.

When the glue is dry, but before it has set hard—usually within twenty-four hours—the books are ready for rounding and backing.

The purpose of rounding is to ensure that the finished book keeps it shape and that the fore-edge is protected as it is not allowed to project forward beyond the cover. It consists in giving the back of the book a convex shape and—reasonably enough—this produces a concave finish for the fore-edge. The amount of rounding given to a book usually depends on the particular characteristics of both paper and sewing and it is usually desirable to avoid an excessive rounding as this not only wastes the margin of the centre signatures but also tends to make the book difficult to open near the centre. It is generally agreed that the rounding of any book should not exceed one-third of a circle.

The machine used for the rounding of a book also backs them. Backing is the process whereby the spine is hammered, rolled or pressed over from the centre signatures so that a small ridge is produced at right angles to the front and back of the book. It serves the very necessary purpose in a hand-cased book of providing an effective joint for the cloth of the covered case between the boards and the spine, and it also serves to keep the boards in position. With rounding it ensures that the book maintains its curve by turning the edges of the sections so that they are locked together, and perhaps most important of all, the combined processes give the pages a hinge by creasing them near the spine so that the book opens and lies open easily.

All this is achieved by a fairly simple but heavily made machine, usually called a roller-backer for smaller editions or a rounding and backing machine for the larger runs. The machine consists of a spring-loaded clamp which grips the book back uppermost and passes it along to two rollers rotating in opposite directions above a cylindrical form against which the rollers press the fore-edge of the book, and so force up the centre section as the outer sections are drawn down by the rollers. The rounded book passes on to a concave roller which presses down on and then moves from side to side across the spine of the tightly clamped book, so giving the spine a smooth roundness and pressing the back edges of the sections over from the centre.

There is a wide range of machines for rounding and backing, and the type of machine described is in use today in most large edition binderies. The smaller machine—a roller-backer—consists essentially of a jig to enable the bookbinder to carry out the two processes quickly and efficiently.

The lining machine carries out a simple series of operations, but it is a surprisingly complex piece of machinery consisting of six stations to each of which books are carried by conveyors. At the first the book is glued up, and it then moves on to a point where the mull is stuck on after it has been trimmed by the machine to the appropriate size, which is usually about a quarter of an inch short of the length of the book and with an overlap of half to three-quarters of an inch for the sides of the book. At the next station the mull is pressed down, and the book is then glued up again without allowing any glue to come into contact with the mull overlap, and the book passes on to the final station, where the soft lining paper already cut to fit is pressed firmly on to the back. The mull serves to reinforce the joint made by the endpapers, and without mull or some effective substitute for mull the book would lack strength. The lining paper is strong, soft and flexible, and when affixed to the spine it stops the book opening too quickly and ensures that the back of the finished book maintains a smooth appearance.

During the time that the forwarding processes have been going on a parallel series of processes have been carried out to produce the case to cover and protect the book. The case-making machine is set up either from dummies of the correct size or from a few copies of the book taken through the various earlier forwarding processes quite separately. As with most of the bookbinding machines of today, the case-making machines suitable for small runs are British, and the high-speed, fully automatic machines are usually American.

Our concern at this stage is with the faster machine, and these are of two types—the Smyth and the Sheridan—the Smyth requires the cloth to be cut into pieces of the required sizes and with corners properly trimmed before it is fed into the machine. The Sheridan case-maker cuts and trims the cloth as part of the process, but it is interesting to note that the apparent disadvantage of the first type of case-making is an advantage when it comes to producing a case of two different cloths or in two different colours —a not unusual modern practice.

The Smyth machine is fully automatic, but can be quickly converted to hand feeding. This is the type of machine that uses covers already cut to size by which is meant the cloth cutter allows half an inch all round for turn-in and trims the corners. The strawboard for the case is placed in two separate containers at the back of the machine, and below these two containers lies the reel of lining paper for the spine or for the back hollow. The machine begins the chain of operations by picking up a piece of cut cloth, feeding it on to a gluing cylinder, and then carrying it on to a sloping platform in the centre of the machine, where the boards and hollow back are placed on it exactly in position. As the case moves along the platform a series of ingeniously cammed bars turn in the cloth at fore-edges and head and tail, and the case then passes into a press made up of a water jacket and a rubber blanket which squeezes out any ripples before discharging the case into a piling trough.

The Sheridan machine differs in that whereas the Smyth operates on a rotary principle the Sheridan follows the straight-line method of production. The two machines also differ in that the Sheridan feeds cloth from a roll slit to the proper width, and the pieces are then cut into appropriate lengths and the corners are turned in after the boards have been placed on the glued roll of cloth. It is a faster and more expensive machine.

The cases are now ready for blocking or printing, and for this purpose a fully automatic blocking press is normally used, working with either gold, coloured or metal foil, or in blind. This finishing press operates on the principle of a platen, but where the area to be blocked is fairly large a much heavier embossing press is called into use. For most of the work today three stamps are cut in quarter-inch brass by a highly skilled stamp cutter. These stamps are produced in fine relief to the lettering and design laid down by the book typographer, and the finished product must have a clearly cut and polished surface before it is locked in the blocking press, where it is heated up to the required temperature by a thermostatically controlled heating element. The heated block or blocks are brought into contact with the case which has been fed on to the solid platform if the work is to be done in blind, otherwise the coloured foil or gold-leaf is fed in rolls

77

between the heated block and the case. The colour or gold is heated and impressed on the case at the correct temperature—if there is any marked variation in temperature the finishing becomes either patchy if it is too low, or smudgy if it is too hot. The platen-type press can also be used with inking rollers, but it is more usual for this class of work to use a small printing press specially adapted for printing covers and using a specially prepared ink that will stand the heavy pressure involved.

The case is now complete and the work on the body of the book has been proceeding simultaneously so that the two are ready to be joined together by the casing machine.

There are three types of machine. The hand-fed rather slow machine which carries out the process one book at a time; the rather faster semi-automatic machine which carries three books in various stages at any time; and the fully automatic machine which deals at a fairly high speed with six books at any one time.

This last machine, the Smyth new style, operates on a rotary principle with six blades adjusted to six processing stations. After the uncased book has been fed into the machine it is led by pairs of control grippers to a blade inserted in the centre of the text of the book which carries the book to a pair of paste feeds which give a thorough pasting to the endpapers, the mull overlaps and the tapes, and by an ingenious device the paster gives a heavier layer at the spine edge. Meanwhile the case has been moving round at a slightly higher level, and after it has been fanned it is carried by a blade to paste feeds and then at the final stations the pasted book is raised into the parted case and pressed well down by clamps which seize it below the joints, and then turn it over before it is fed into the chute for the binder to check the squares before passing it for a final pressing.

Effective adhesion is only secured by continuous pressure, and this pressure if it is to be effective must be applied not only to the flat surface of the boards but also to the French joint, as it is at this point that the book when in use will be called upon to bear the greatest strain. To achieve this a specially prepared series of binding boards three-eighths to half an inch thick are used. These rectangular hardwood boards have a brass strip mounted along one length projecting for about one-sixteenth of an inch above the main flat surfaces. These binding boards are placed edge outwards on the base of a wheeled press truck, and the first layer of books is then laid on so that the gap between the board and spine coincide with the brass projection. A further layer of binding boards is then fitted over the top of the first layer of books, and these are themselves covered with a second layer of books, and so on until the press truck is full, when the top plate is then fitted on and screwed down before being wheeled to the pneumatic press, which applies some 70 pounds per square inch pressure, whereupon the truck press is fastened to hold the pressure and then wheeled away to stand overnight.

Pressure is taken off the following day, and the books are then given a quick check before the dust jackets are applied. It is an interesting reflection of machine methods that the application of jackets—apparently the simplest of a whole series of complex operations—is still carried out almost entirely by hand, although it is believed that a machine has recently been manufactured for this purpose and is now being marketed.

CHAPTER EIGHT

Commercial library binderies

It CAN be estimated that the library binderies attached to public libraries have an annual output of less than 200,000 re-bound volumes per annum. It also seems likely that public library authorities in Great Britain and Northern Ireland are spending about three-quarters of a million pounds on re-binding books. Assuming that the average cost of rebinding a book is 6s. 8d., it will be seen that approximately 2,250,000 volumes are re-bound annually, and of these more than 2,000,000 volumes are bound by commercial library binders.

The binders doing this work fall into two fairly broad categories. There is the group of old-established undertakings specializing in library bookbinding, and a second group of smaller firms ranging from the craft shop which does not as a rule specialize in library binding to the recently established bindery occasionally using new techniques, such as unsewn binding, but more often relying on a slightly lower price and usually producing a slightly inferior binding to that of the larger binders. In short, there is a reasonably sound economic network which ensures that prices and production are kept at competitive levels.

Our concern in this chapter is with the organization and variations in technique which have been adopted by the group of larger undertakings who bind by far the greater part of the books re-bound for public libraries. The fact that the group has a membership of probably four and not more than six firms should not be taken to imply that these old-established companies are complacent as the competition between them is strong and the purchasers of the finished commodity are reasonably discriminating.

The librarian requires his bookbinder to produce a re-bound book which will: (i) open easily and keep its shape after repeated openings; (ii) be fairly durable and just outlast the text of the book; (iii) be attractively and appropriately bound; (iv) be reasonably cheap; (v) be produced in a factory where fair working conditions are maintained. Apart from the last of these requirements the remainder tend to a certain extent to be in conflict with each other, but the modern commercial binder has adjusted his output to the needs of the library service and has achieved a nicely balanced compromise so that, for example, a crown octavo fiction title is re-bound by mass-production methods which eliminate the expensive processes designed to produce a more permanent binding, but he can, on the other hand, also carry out a careful restoration in the best traditions of English binding.

It is generally laid down by writers and lecturers on library administration that a series of model specifications for all classes of books are necessary and to provide a basis for such specifications the joint recommendations of the American Library Association and the Library Binding Institute for Class A Library Binding are published in Appendix II by permission of the Library Binding Institute. These recommendations, it will be found, break away from the well-established convention that all library bindings should have, for example, a specially constructed zig-zag endpaper and that no books should have less than three tapes. If these Class A Library Binding specifications are examined carefully they will be found to provide an interesting outline of differing practices in the two countries and a sound basis for a procedure to be followed by the librarian. At the same time, as one of our leading commercial bookbinders has stated: "One has to remember that proper bookbinding all depends upon the goodwill of the bookbinder and the measure of his desire to give a sound job, and without this the most rigid specifications avail nothing." This same firm of bookbinders themselves issue a general specification for library bookbinding as follows:

(i) The standard of reinforcement of sections is for guarding with serrated edge paper.

(ii) Endpapers incorporate a cloth joint.

(iii) Books sewn with linen or nylon thread of adequate strength.

(iv) Books sewn on tapes varying in number according to size and weight of paper.

(v) Oversewing used only in those instances where other methods are impracticable.

(vi) All plates, maps, etc., guarded into the text, except in those instances where they can be more suitably folded and placed in a pocket constructed on the inside of the back board of the book.

(vii) The edges of all books trimmed and sprinkled with one neutral colour.

(viii) Boards of adequate thickness for the size and weight of the book.

(ix) Boards split to receive tapes and cloth joints of all heavy and large books.

(x) Book backs strongly lined.

(xi) Books covered in fast finish cloth or buckram (according to size and weight of book) in our selected range of colours. "Acid free and protected" leather used where specified.

(xii) Bright non-tarnishing foil used for lettering the three smallest sizes of fiction and non-fiction books bound in cloth and buckram. All other books lettered with real gold.

(xiii) Pockets and labels inserted where supplied.

(xiv) The size of the book determined by the measurement of the length of the board from head to tail, and the width of the book from the backing-joint to the fore-edge of the board after binding.

(xv) Intermediate sizes charged at the next largest size.

(xvi) Books greater in thickness than one-half their respective board widths charged at 50 per cent more than the schedule price.

(xvii) Prices quoted are subject to revision in the event of an increase in the cost of materials or rise in wages rates negotiated in the bookbinding industry.

This specification is in fact merely a general outline of the procedure followed by this undertaking and could hardly be described as a detailed specification. Nevertheless it serves to underline the difficulties inherent in making a detailed specification, and it will be seen, for example, that in the matter of the thread to be used the trade specification is more specific than the Class A specification. Even so, no attempt is made to lay down the particular thickness of thread which is to be used for a book as this would obviously depend on the weight and strength of paper and the size of the book. Nevertheless an inappropriate thickness of thread would ruin a binding, however closely it followed the specification, and it would therefore seem reasonable to compile and revise regularly a detailed specification on the lines of the Class A specification as a general guide to both librarians and bookbinders. Such a specification would not guarantee a high standard of workmanship, but it would serve to show librarians how to organize their bookbinding so that bookbinders could give the best possible service, and it would indicate to bookbinders certain minimum standards below which they must not fall.

The procedure followed in all these binderies is fairly similar, and it is proposed to give a composite picture of production methods with particular emphasis on those which differ from the library bindery or the craft binder on the one hand and the edition binder on the other, as it will be understood that commercial library bindery procedure is a compromise between these two techniques.

CHECKING

The books are usually collected at regular intervals by the bookbinder's own transport, and on arrival at the bindery they are checked against any detailed lists or against the summary of the consignment. The consignment is then usually divided into four categories, each of which call for some small variations in production, and these are: (i) conventional crown octavo fiction to be bound to a highly standardized specification; (ii) other sizes of fiction; (iii) conventional non-fiction; (iv) periodicals, newspapers and other special binding which is the subject of detailed standing instructions or for which special instructions are issued.

Books in categories (i) and (ii) are given a batch number and a mark of ownership and passed through to the next stage. Books in category (iii) are occasionally listed if no list has been received from the librarian and a work slip giving special instructions as to style, material, colour and finishing is placed inside the book.

Works in category (iv) call for special treatment, and in addition to work slips a docket containing a list of the works to be bound, any rubbings of previous volumes and detailed instructions is attached to the work to accompany it throughout the various processes.

From this point on the work proceeds through the factory passing from process to process and being subjected to occasional checks. In the case of special binding these checks are carried out as a means of drawing the batch of books together, but as it is the practice either to bring forward particular categories of books at one time or in the case of the larger factories to have separate production lines, this presents few difficulties.

Bearing this procedure in mind, it would seem to be reasonable today for the librarian to send all fiction to the bindery without a detailed covering list, but merely to state the total number of volumes dispatched. Non-fiction requiring special treatment needs a checking list, and if the librarian does not provide it the bookbinder must. A detailed list provided by the librarian will ensure that the work is done both in accordance with the library's normal practice and that the volumes of one work are bound uniformly. Such a list should give the style of binding required; the colour if a particular colour is required; the title and author as it is to appear in the spine; the class number and author mark, and any extra work such as gilt fillets, raised bands, or to conform to pattern. Without such a list the bookbinder will do the best he can, and the result will usually be indistinguishable from the result achieved with the carefully compiled list, but inevitably without a list from the librarian small mistakes will creep in. Newspapers, periodicals and similar material should be the subject of a detailed initial order, specifying exactly what is wanted in such matters as the inclusion of advertisements, the precise style of binding, and the colour. The bookbinder will file the instructions and subsequently take and file a rubbing so that further volumes will be bound in exact conformity and present no further problems for the librarian. It should be added at this point that librarians and bookbinders could with advantage establish a standard code of practice for the lettering and numbering of bound sets of periodicals.

Occasionally a librarian will give a general instruction regarding all books bound for him such as the not unusual instruction that no book should be oversewn without special permission being given, or it may be that a particular type or colour of cloth is not to be used. Such instructions are carried out as far as possible, but it will be realized that with the development of mass-production techniques it is no longer possible to isolate particular volumes, particularly if these volumes are crown octavo fiction being bound at a cheap rate.

PULLING

The covers of the book are then pulled off and the spine of the book is given a preliminary scraping with a knife to remove old glue. The sewing is then cut out in a laborious hand process which apparently defies any mechanical simplification because of the variations in styles of publishers' sewing, pages per section, thickness of page and the shape of the back. The sections are pulled away and the final remnants of the old glue removed. The book now having been reduced to sections, it is carefully collated by both signatures and leaves, the illustrations are checked, and an assessment made and indications given by flagging each book's particular requirements for repair. Imperfect and damaged books are withdrawn for a decision as to their future by the librarian, or they are returned to the librarian as unsuitable for binding.

REPAIRING AND REINFORCING

The majority of books coming into the hands of the commercial library binder are inevitably in publishers' cases, as it is as unusual as it is uneconomic to re-bind books previously subjected to a library binding, except in special circumstances. The majority of books in publishers' cases have received an average of thirty or more issues, and many of them are slightly soiled and a little damaged. Basing his decision on the type of book and the style of binding, the commercial library binder decides on the extent of the repairs to be carried out. Cleaning and repairs are expensive items, and it is not the practice to carry out elaborate stain-removing processes or to make repairs of a book due to receive a cheap binding. Such books are either returned to the librarian or passed through for the conventional processes. Such repairs as are carried out for conventional binding are usually limited to making good torn pages with transparent tissue.

It would be futile to provide a strong hard-wearing binding with tipped-in illustrations, and all single-leaf illustrations are guarded so that they can be sewn in.

Inevitably the books in publishers' cases are most in need of repair at the folds, where the previous use of the book has tended to enlarge the original sewing holes and the pulling down of the book has damaged the folds even further.

A fairly general practice today is to reinforce each pair of leaves with a strip of gummed tissue paper varying in width from half to three-quarters of an inch and occasionally used with a serrated edge. In addition the first pair of leaves in the first and last sections of each book are reinforced with linen tape, or the cloth reinforcement used for the endpaper is carried through to these sections.

The procedure used for reinforcing the books in this way is fairly simple, consisting of a roll of tape fed over a damp roller. The tape is then pressed down on one side only of the fold of the pair of leaves and trimmed with a simple hand guillotine. In one factory the process has been rather ingeniously mechanized as the leaves are placed on a platform by a girl operator, and they are then carried forward, reinforced from a continuous roll of moistened gummed tape and then trimmed roughly to size.

It will be noticed that it is often the practice to reinforce the fold of pairs of leaves on one side only in such a way that the outer side of the first fold of each section and the inner side of the last fold of each section is reinforced and in the rest of the section the reinforcement alternates between the front and the back of each pair of leaves. This would seem to be an excellent practice, giving effective reinforcement without excessive swelling in most cases.

NIPPING AND SEWING

When the sections have been reinforced the spine is inevitably swollen, and a book shaped in this way would present considerable difficulties to the bookbinder in all subsequent forwarding processes. The problem has been overcome by the introduction of a book nipping machine, which squeezes the spines to a predetermined thickness by pressing the reinforcing paper tape into the softer text paper and leaves the book with sufficient swelling at the spine to allow for the rounding and backing which is to follow in due course.

For at least forty years machine sewing has been replacing hand sewing in commercial library binderies, and today the book-sewing machine has reached such a degree of perfection that only the occasional book of irregular size, the file of newspapers or the volume of periodicals is hand sewn.

Before the sewing begins endpapers are prepared and these usually consist of a strong calendered cover paper with a broad linen reinforcement on either the inner or outer fold. Special endpapers are prepared, including additional fly-leaves, for special bindings, but these vary considerably with the practice of the house and the requirements of the particular volume.

The machine-sewn book is in every way satisfactory for the majority of library books as such a book is sewn cheaply, strongly and evenly, and the book is not mutilated in any way. The present practice of the binders is to sew round tapes, but one of the larger binders has abandoned tapes for the conventional cheap binding of smaller volumes, and sews directly on to a superior quality mull. Nylon thread has been introduced to replace the cotton and linen threads used on certain sewing machines, and it is claimed that the strength and consistency of nylon when used on these machines give a result equal to other sewing threads. More recently Terylene thread has been used, and this would appear to be very suitable for book sewing.

Endpapers are sewn through at the beginning of each book, and all sections are then sewn together with the illustrations inserted at the appropriate place and the guards folded in so that these too are sewn through. Each book finishes with an endpaper which is sewn in, and the book is removed as one of a continuous block linked by tapes round which the sewing has passed. The tapes are adjusted to give an overlap of half to three-quarters of an inch at the back and front of the volume, and the continuous thread and tapes are cut and trimmed. Finally the projecting strips of tape are given a touch of paste and pressed down on to the endpaper.

Sewing also serves to swell out the spine of the book, and before any further processes can be carried out this swelling is reduced in the book nipping press. A nice judgement is called for in this process if the book is to be reduced to a reasonably workable shape without forcing the thread through the paper.

After nipping, the book is glued up with a coating of flexible glue applied by a machine equipped with rotating brushes which operate against the spine of the clamped book in such a way as to ensure that the glue is well brushed into the joins of the sections. In some binderies the book is then lined up with a piece of mull which projects half an inch over the front and back of the book and allowed to dry out sufficiently to ensure that it will maintain a good shape, but not so dry that it will subsequently be difficult to round and back.

TRIMMING AND SPRAYING

A guillotine is used for trimming, and in the case of the cheaper routine binding it is the practice to trim the edges of the book down to one of a wide range of standard sizes, but with other work the edges are trimmed down to take off the barest minimum from the edge of the page. The machine used is usually a three-edge trimmer in which one blade descends and trims the fore-edge of the tightly clamped books, and then two further blades descend at right angles to trim the head and tail. If the margin available for trimming is extremely narrow a sanding machine is used in some factories, and this rubs off the edge quickly and efficiently with a minimum of work.

The edges of the books are now usually sprayed with continuous colour, although occasionally it is the practice to sprinkle the edges with colour. The spraying is carried out by means of a high-pressure colour spray in a quick-drying cupboard, and as with sprinkling it is applied to a column of books at a time. The purpose of this edge colouring is threefold in that it prevents the edges from showing any soiling during subsequent bookbinding processes; it maintains the appearance of the book during its useful life, and it occasionally improves the appearance of the book. It is, of course, difficult when mass-production techniques are being used to match the colour of the edge spraying with the final cover of the book and the colour of foil used on that cover, and the use of neutral shades tends to give the book an institutional appearance.

ROUNDING AND BACKING

Competition between commercial library binders inevitably results in a demand for new labour-saving machinery that will lower production costs without any lowering of the standard of the finished product. One of the most significant advances of this type has been the fully automatic self-centring rounder and backer, and this is now largely replacing the semi-automatic rounder and backer which is still used in more or less the original design first marketed at the beginning of the century. The fully automatic rounder and backer is an ingenious machine which picks up and presses forward the spine of the book so that the sections are pressed outward and away from the centre section, and then presses the outer section over to make a projection at right angles to the front and back pages of the book in such a way that the boards will subsequently hinge and fit neatly. The book is now nicely shaped, having been given a spine with a curve adjusted to the thickness of the book.

CASING

From this point it is necessary to make a rather clearer distinction between the methods adopted for crown octavo fiction binding and the binding of other types of library books, as in most commercial binderies production is divided into two quite distinct streams. The principal difference comes in the making of the case, which is made quite independently of the book in a wide variety of sizes for a crown octavo, and subsequently taken "off the peg" and fitted to the book, which has been previously trimmed down to one of the standard sizes. The forwarding of other classes of books proceeds more in accordance with the practice of the craft binder than that of the edition binder.

The machine used for making crown octavo cases is usually a Smyth case-making machine similar to that described in the chapter on the making of a book, although one of the larger

89

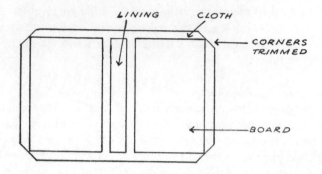

THE CASE LAID-OUT

binders has used a smaller machine with a fair measure of success. The machine is fed with a good quality strawboard cut to one of the standard sizes with a fairly heavy cover paper for lining up the spine, and with pieces of good quality, stain-resistant library cloth. Using this machine, a large reserve of each size of ready-made case is maintained in batches of assorted colours so that every consignment of books contains a reasonable assortment of colours. Books are then brought forward in batches of the same standard size, and they are carefully fitted into cases.

Meanwhile the alternative method of casing is carried on, either by making up split boards by the partial gluing together of one thin and one thick board or by actually splitting the edge of a fairly thick board to a depth of one and a half inches or so. The split boards having been carefully cut to size, the glue is applied to two sides of the split before laying in the tab carrying the tapes, and so fastening the boards firmly to the book. The book is subsequently subjected to pressure so that it dries out a little. It seems reasonable that boards affixed in this way give a stronger binding than the casing method used for crown octavo, but it also seems reasonable to add that for most books designed for current use in home reading libraries a well-made cased book is sufficiently strong and durable and retains its shape almost as well as the more carefully bound book.

The book with its split boards then comes from the standing press, the squares of the boards are adjusted, and when the book

90

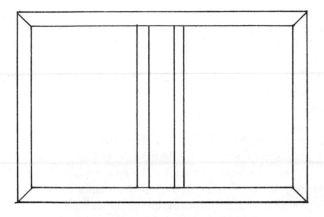

THE CASE TURNED-IN

is to be bound with a hollow back—and the majority of books are so bound—a lining of fairly thick and porous cover paper is glued on to the spine of the book and made into a tube, thus giving a segmental hollow round in which the cover of the spine can lie and retain its shape. Rather surprisingly this is a process which it has not been found possible to rationalize in any way, and it remains the general practice actually to construct the tube on the spine of each book.

Cloth or leather or both have been cut to size, and this is now glued and drawn on to the back, fastened down into the joints and pressed over the edges by means of a bone folder. The book is then returned to the press, where it remains for at least twelve hours.

Probably the most significant change in library binding has been the steady replacement of leather by cloth. Leather—all of it PIRA tested—is still widely used, particularly for certain classes of reference binding and newspaper and periodical binding. In spite of an attractive range of colours it is now relatively little used for the binding of home reading library books. The reason for this change is not merely that leather is much more expensive than cloth, but that cloth is now manufactured in bright colours with many finishes and is stain-resistant.

FINISHING

The lettering, numbering and decoration of a re-bound book is the most expensive of the various processes, and although the basic technique of applying heated letters through a coloured or metallic transfer have not been changed the equipment and materials in use have changed considerably in the past twenty-five years.

The most significant step was the introduction of the type-setting machine in place of the hand-selected and assembled brass letters. These machines—of which the Linotype and the Intertype are the best known—are similar to the machines used in many printing-offices, and they are used to produce a slug for each title. The operator sits at his machine with the cased books fanned open and standing on their edges round a revolving table. Each batch of books has a batch of slugs produced for it, and these are carried off to the finisher. The advantage of such a process is not merely that it is cheaper but that it also produces new, fairly sharp-edged type for each book. Even so, the older technique of assembling type in a hand-pallet is occasionally used for the book of irregular size.

The crown octavo books are, however, still loose in their cases, and for these slugs are also made. The finisher who is handling these smaller books is now equipped in some binderies with a complicated type of blocking press which is loaded with the appropriate Linotype or Intertype slug, and he then brings the heated slug into contact with the spine of the case through a metallic or coloured transfer, so giving an evenness and a clarity of outline which the human wrist and hand cannot achieve. After this the lettered case is fixed to the book by pasting the inner surface of the case, the projecting tapes or mull and the appropriate surfaces of the endpapers. All of which are pressed together and the book is then left to dry in a standing press. It has been found that a strong and effective joint can be produced in this way. However, the blocking machine is not a complete answer, and a large proportion of the books bound in our library binderies today are lettered by means of Linotype or Intertype slugs in a hand-pallet as they needs must be if the case is an integral part of the book.

The medium used for this lettering varies from gold-leaf to the various coloured foils. Gold-leaf is rather expensive, but to many librarians and to many bookbinders it continues to be quite the best finishing medium. Recently advances have been made with a non-tarnishing aluminium foil which gives a sharp, glowing, silvery finish and which appears to be quite satisfactory. Coloured foils were widely used by commercial library binders for the first time after the last war, but showed a tendency to fade and rub off when exposed to dampness. This has been overcome, and apart from a tendency to use coloured foils which lie rather unhappily with the colour of the cover these foils have now proved themselves to be quite satisfactory being both cheap and hard-wearing.

GENERAL

It would be misleading to conclude this outline of the processes used in the commercial library binderies without giving some fuller indication of the range of services given by these undertakings. Certainly their principal business is the rebinding of crown octavo fiction, conventional non-fiction, extra size fiction and newspapers and periodicals, but all these binderies are conscious of the craft traditions upon which their techniques are based. Although it is neither possible nor desirable for such factories to upset production with craft binding many of them are prepared to undertake occasional special commissions to produce fine binding. Many of them are also prepared to undertake the repair, restoration or rebinding of books which require considerable individual and special treatment. It would be a great loss not only to the craft of bookbinding if these skills are ever completely lost, and it may be that today's librarians can and should occasionally commission work of this kind.

In addition the commercial library binders offer a wide range of services in the binding and protection of special material. There is, for example, the binding of music in many styles and there is also an excellent pamphlet binding service. The mounting of maps, the reinforcing of individual copies of sets of plays and their protection with a titled slip case, and the provision of magazine cases are but a few of the special services given.

The public libraries of Great Britain are fortunate in the commercial library binderies that serve them for the service they give is both competitive and of a consistently high standard. It may be that the future will demand a considerable change in the output of these factories from the conventional home reading binding to the more difficult problem of special storage and reference binding on the one hand, to reinforcement and the use of plastic films on the other. Should such a change come it will demand enterprising production methods based upon sound research and practical experience.

Certainly whatever the future holds in this particular field closer co-operation between librarians and commercial bookbinders is called for. There may not be room in this country for an organization as active and as useful as the Library Binding Institute of America, but there is surely a great deal to be said for representatives on both sides meeting occasionally to discuss problems of common interest.

CHAPTER NINE

The library bindery: its organization, administration and economics

IN 1911 Henry T. Coutts wrote in *Library Bookbinding* that: "A Home Bindery or Book Repairing Department is becoming generally recognised as an essential part of the administration of the larger public library systems. . . . Such binderies are only applicable to large library systems where a big turnover of bookbinding justifies the expense involved in buying the necessary appliances and materials and paying the wages of qualified work people."

Prior to 1911, library binderies had been established at Aberdeen, Brighton, Bristol, Derby, Hull and Portsmouth. Since that date binderies have also been opened by a number of other authorities, including Croydon, Durham, Lambeth, Leeds, Manchester, Nottingham, Plymouth, Stoke, Tottenham and East Suffolk. Dagenham started a bindery in 1935 and closed it in 1941, only to reopen it again a few years later.

In fifty years of fairly energetic propaganda in favour of library binderies some sixteen authorities have in fact established them. That such a small number have been established may be due to the innate conservatism of librarians and the authorities they serve, or it may be due to the conviction that the work can be more economically and efficiently carried out by commercial binders.

It is the purpose of this chapter to enable the practising librarian to consider the organization, administration and economics of a library bindery in fairly general terms so that he can then approach the problem in the light of his local problems and local requirements.

First it must be recognized that although there are sixteen or so library binderies they vary considerably in their output, costs and equipment, but it would seem to be practicable and convenient to divide them into three categories: (i) the library bindery specializing in conventional library binding and producing 20,000 or more bound books per annum—there are five such binderies; (ii) the combined repair shop and bindery which binds more than 10,000 books a year and also carries out a good deal of specialized work, including repairs, restoration, binding of special material, making of boxes and display fittings, the restoration of maps—there are three or four such binderies; (iii) the repair shop, which is not concerned principally with rebinding, although some rebinding is carried out, but specializes in the additional work detailed in (ii) above—there are seven or more of these repair shops.

It is proposed to consider only those library binderies falling in categories (i) and (ii).

The justification for the establishment of a library bindery will vary with its size and purpose in relation to the needs of the particular authority, but the following general arguments in favour of library binderies are those usually advanced: (a) that if the library system is large enough it can bind books more cheaply and quite as effectively as the commercial library bindery; (b) that the needs of the library service can be met most effectively by a bindery working under the administrative supervision of a librarian as this will ensure a balanced production related to the varying needs of the service; (c) that the binder will not require detailed instructions but will work with a clear knowledge of the particular library background, and will so choose appropriate materials and techniques within the directives given to him by the administration; (d) that the book stock at the bindery is readily available to meet urgent requests; (e) that the preparation of detailed lists by library staff is not necessary and the subsequent checking of books against invoices is also avoided; (f) that a great deal of additional work such as the numbering and labelling of books, the making of special boxes, display fittings, and readers' tickets can be carried out economically in the bindery, and (g) that it provides employment locally.

All of which are countered to some extent by arguments against the establishment of a library bindery, and these are: (a) that only a large library system can hope to provide such a workshop on an economic basis; (*b*) the bookbinding staff must be of a high calibre, and bookbinding staff of any calibre are difficult to obtain; (*c*) that the initial expenditure is high and accommodation is often expensive and also difficult to obtain; (*d*) that commercial library binders do not now require lists and books required urgently can usually be returned within seven days; (*e*) that the establishment, administration and general supervision of a library bindery cannot be efficiently undertaken by most librarians, and where it can be so undertaken it must inevitably result both in fairly prolonged and relatively unproductive teething troubles, and also in the librarian and his staff being diverted from the main task of directing a library service, and (*f*) that the standard of routine binding produced by the library bindery is generally inferior to that produced by the commercial firms.

All of which might be summarized with the statement that a library bindery can be a fairly considerable convenience, but the convenience is not such that it will offset any marked increase in costs when compared with the commercial bindery.

Unfortunately the issue of relative costs is not capable of a direct and simple answer as few library authorities cost the work of the library bindery in any detail, and where it is costed the figures are usually weighted in favour of the bindery as they do not normally include overheads such as a proportion of the administrative expenses for the supervisory and office work carried out by the librarian and his staff. The average cost of binding books commercially is known for a number of municipal library systems, and it would appear to be between 4*s*. 6*d*. and 5*s*. 6*d*., depending on the amount of special work such as newspaper and periodical binding. The average cost of binding a volume in a library bindery ranges from 4*s*. to 6*s*., but it is noteworthy that in those library binderies with a turnover in excess of 20,000 volumes per annum the average cost is 4*s*. 3*d*. When the capital expenditure and the methods of costing are born in mind, it will be seen that the issue of whether to provide a library bindery is nicely balanced.

It would be most useful at this stage to consider the output, equipment, staffing and general organization and administration of the larger type of library bindery as the pattern is fairly

97

similar for all binderies concerned with the large-scale binding of books.

The organization of the book flow calls for some care as it is necessary to ensure that the books to be bound should be fed in at such a rate that on the one hand the bindery is not choked with books, and on the other it must not be so limited that there is not an adequate reserve to enable the books to be matched up in sizes and to a certain extent matched up by title. It has been found that a reserve of 10 per cent of the total annual production can usually be carried most efficiently from a production point of view; this may be rather too large as it necessitates a delay of more than a month before each book is bound, but the advantage of a bindery with an output of 40,000 books per annum carrying a reserve of 4,000 volumes is that such a reserve often produces sets of the same title and allows adequate sizing.

The staffing of a library bindery is the real key to its effectiveness. It demands before anything else the services of a skilled and conscientious foreman who is not only capable of working with little pressure and supervision from above, but can also command from the bindery staff both industry and loyalty. Rare qualities all these, but without such a man a library bindery can easily become both an extravagance for the authority and an administrative burden for the librarian. Given such a man, it should be recognized that his responsibilities and talents merit special pay, and an appropriate merit bonus above the usual rates should be paid.

It is then necessary to build up a balanced team of craftsmen and women that will be sufficiently large to allow for sickness and holidays without serious disruption of production. A finisher can letter 15,000 home reading books a year, and the most satisfactory team will obviously start with two such finishers giving a basic annual output of 30,000 volumes. To forward this number of books five forwarders are required and nine sewers, if we assume that the bindery is fairly well equipped with machinery. This gives a team of seventeen including the foreman, and is based on the assump ion that extra work will be carried out by the foreman as required, and that each forwarder will produce 6,000 volumes a year and each girl or woman will pull down, collate, repair and sew 3,333 volumes a year—an average annual output for each member of the staff of 1,765 volumes.

This question of the number of workpeople is all important, and if it were to be accepted that a unit producing 30,000 bound books a year was the smallest efficient economic unit it would follow that only those library authorities issuing about 3,000,000 books a year could consider the establishment of a library bindery. It is believed that such a unit or a larger unit is the most effective, but it is also believed that a smaller unit can still function with a sufficient margin to make it economically worth while, and from the information available it would seem that about 20,000 volumes re-bound annually is the smallest output which can be competitively bound by a library bindery. Given this figure as the lowest effective production, it would seem that the staffing should be one foreman binder, one finisher, three forwarders and seven sewers—a staff of twelve with an average annual output of 1,666 volumes.

In providing the equipment for a bindery of this size it is necessary to introduce machinery wherever the return justifies it. For example, a sewing machine costs approximately £900 and can be assumed for depreciation purposes to have a life of ten years. The cost of electricity for such a machine is about £5–6 a year when it is used to sew 30,000 books. Sewing this number of books by hand would probably require fifteen girls or women at a cost of £2,000 per annum. With a machine it is possible to sew this number of books with a labour force of nine girls at an annual cost of £1,150. Allowing for electricity and depreciation and making no allowance for the saving of floor space this produces an annual saving of £755. This fairly considerable saving is effected in spite of only using the machine for half the working hours. It might of course be argued that the introduction of such machinery into a craft produces an inferior book, but if the sewing machine is being properly used for binding most of the books needed for the average public library, it will be found that the sewing lasts the useful life of the books, and this is the essential test.

No library bindery can operate economically without a guillotine. The machine used usually consists of an electrically powered single-edge guillotine with a 38-inch blade, giving a 32-inch cut and costing from £500 to £600. Such a machine if carefully chosen should give twenty years' wear before it needs overhauling, and during this period it should give a fine, smooth-cut surface and should be able to trim down to a thirty-second of an inch. The hand-operated guillotine can still be found in use in library binderies, but the strain of operating it, the noise produced by it and the relative lack of precision make a power-operated guillotine a necessary piece of machinery.

A smaller piece of machinery is occasionally provided in order to cut boards, but the more usual equipment is the long-handled shearing knife like a specially mounted photographic trimmer. However, some of the stronger all-purpose, power-operated guillotines can be used for this task when the cutting of boards in bulk is called for.

The rounder backer is fairly fully described in the chapter on the making of a book. This machine is essential for the large library bindery producing 30,000 books a year, but owing to the variation in book sizes that occurs in a library bindery it has been found that the amount of adjustment is such that a rounder backer would produce little saving in a smaller bindery.

In the forwarding processes a considerable saving in labour costs can be effected by the introduction of a gluing machine. An 18-inch electrically operated whole-surface gluing machine costs about £100, and the speed, the control and the certainty with which the machine can glue cloth for case-making make it an invaluable piece of equipment in a bindery with an output of 20,000 or more volumes per annum.

Another ingenious machine which can save forwarding time is a 24-inch turning-in machine. At a cost of just over £100 this machine folds the glued cloth and then presses it over on to the board, forming an effective and nicely made cover. A simple operation carried out by a fairly simple machine, but it saves time and soon saves its cost.

The process of lettering has not yet been satisfactorily mechanized, but a moderately priced lettering machine with a fairly simple action consisting of an engraved and heated wheel which is applied to the book mounted in a carriage is now being marketed and may prove to be the answer. In the meantime the library bindery continues to use the blocking press and the hand-pallet. The lettering is usually set up in brass type, but a number of binderies are using specially cast slugs set up by Linotype or Intertype, and it has also been found that a special hand alloy type can now be specially cast on Monotype, and so give the binder a range of type faces which he has badly needed, even though the type is not so hard-wearing as brass type.

The blocking press has been much improved in recent years, and the heavy platen-type press has been modified so that it can be more easily adjusted and fed, and is fairly simple in operation. The metal typeholder for such a press is rather like a small printer's chase, and after the type has been set up and locked the typeholder slides into the fixed block at the top of the press, where it is heated and a gold foil is fed from a roll feed and the platen then rises, carrying the book case to be blocked. Such a machine is a great economy whenever small runs of the same title are produced, and it can be used for individual copies with economy and efficiency as it produces an evenness of impression not readily obtainable by the hand pallet.

A small nipping press with a sufficient capacity to take a 12-inch book is a useful piece of machinery, particularly if it is the practice to reinforce the spine and inner joints of certain classes of books rather than rebind them. Such a nipping press is fairly lightly loaded and treadle-operated to give a steady even pressure over a limited area, unlike the major standing presses with which the large library bindery must be generously equipped.

All these pieces of machinery are used to supplement the conventional equipment of the craft bindery, the requirements for which are detailed in the chapter on bookbinding by hand. As would be expected, the smaller the bindery the less justification there is for the more expensive and elaborate machinery, and the larger the bindery the closer it will approach the commercial bindery.

The total cost of such machinery is usually met over a number of years as the production of the bindery increases, but the following list of machinery and its approximate cost gives some impression of the capital expenditure involved for a large library bindery:

	£
Sewing machine	900
Guillotine	550
Board cutter	100
Backing press	90
Nipping press	70
Gluing machine	100
Turning-in machine	100
Blocking press	90
	£2,000

To gain a clearer impression of the total capital expenditure it would be necessary to add the cost of providing very expensive type and tools, together with equipment such as hot plates, glue-pots, benches, shelving and a supply of material. An additional cost of £1,500 for equipment and £1,000 for materials would not be excessive.

The techniques used in most of these binderies are similar in that the current practice is not to bind all books in the conventional sense of fastening individual boards or split boards to the book, and then subsequently covering these boards, but rather to give it a superior casing. This modified technique is used for most of the books bound for the home reading libraries, but not for special classes of work such as large volumes and old bindings. The conventional casing method calls for pulling down, collation, repairing, sewing, gluing up, trimming, rounding and backing and then casing. The individually made cases are fastened to the book by means of pasted down tapes and a reinforced endpaper. This gives a reasonably strong joint quite adequate for normal wear in home reading libraries. It is unnecessarily extravagant to specify split boards with three or more tapes for the vast majority of such books, and it will be seen that the A.L.A. minimum specification for Class A library binding in Appendix II specifies casing-in.

For the rest techniques vary as one would expect with size and the degree of mechanization ranging from the small shop in which all work is done by hand to the bindery with an output of 40,000 volumes.

There are some divisions of opinion as to the desirability of a library bindery doing work other than binding. On the one hand it is held that smooth production is broken down by the introduction of various additional tasks, and on the other that one of the principal arguments in favour of a library bindery is that it can carry out the various tasks and that in any case they are used to fill up the production of the bindery, which however well planned cannot be perfectly balanced.

This miscellaneous work includes repair work, ranging from the mending of a torn page to the restitution of an old binding. The simpler mending is done more efficiently and economically than if it were carried out by assistant librarians, and the convention that junior library staff should be capable of carrying out repairs to a book with loose pages or damaged joints can really only be justified if other and far more effective methods are not readily available. One of the most considerable advantages of a bindery undertaking miscellaneous work is that new books can be adequately prepared by staff trained for the job and provided with the necessary equipment to carry it out efficiently. The pasting in of book plates, book card pockets and date labels, together with lettering the spine of the book in gold, produces a finished book far superior to the book lettered with white or by stick-on label, and it takes from the library staff a tiresome task which they often carry out poorly.

Such work as the making of pamphlet boxes and readers' tickets can usually best be avoided by buying what is wanted from the specializing stationers, but even so the tailor-made document box can be produced far more effectively in the library bindery. Special work such as the reinforcing of maps, the treatment of folding or tipped-in plates can often be carried out by the bindery, and it may be that in the course of the next few years the emphasis will move to reinforcing of inner joints and the lamination of dust jackets on new books, and so effect a considerable reduction in the number of books that require binding.

One of the minor advantages of library binderies is that they provide a link between the craftsman and the librarian. Given ready co-operation this ensures both a changing pattern of production to meet changing requirements and a fairly continuous stream of experiment and development.

Finally such large binderies serve to compete with the commercial binderies by ensuring indirectly that competitive prices are maintained and by providing an alternative binding channel so that prolonged delays or an unreasonable emphasis on particular types of bookbinding can be met.

ECONOMICS

It will be seen from Appendix I that the majority of authorities with binderies producing more than 10,000 bound books a year have been included. Interpreting these figures and other figures available on the more detailed costs and output of a particular library bindery, it would seem that the costs of various classes of library binderies are as follows:

40,000 BOOKS BOUND PER ANNUM	£
Wages	6,000
Materials	2,000
Maintenance	75
Rent	200
Heat, water, light	200
Administration	225
	£8,700

An average cost per volume of 4s. 5¼d.

20,000 BOOKS BOUND PER ANNUM	£
Wages	3,500
Materials	1,250
Maintenance	50
Rent	175
Heat, water, light	150
Administration	200
	£5,325

An average cost per volume of 5s. 4d.

10,000 BOOKS BOUND PER ANNUM	£
Wages	1,900
Materials	750
Maintenance	35
Rent	100
Heat, water, light	100
Administration	175
	£3,060

An average cost per volume of 6s. o¾d.

Such figures can do little more than give a general picture as they must obviously vary with the wage rates of the district; the different sizes of book bound; the class of binding and material, and the amount of non-binding work carried out.

CHAPTER TEN

Binding of special classes of material: newspapers, periodicals, music, pamphlets, maps and the like

NEWSPAPERS

It was in 1861 that Routledge introduced esparto into news-print, but even so the paper made exclusively of rag continued to be used for many newspapers, and it was not until the middle of the First World War that new materials, including mechanical wood and inadequately washed pulp, were introduced. The conse-quent deterioration of newsprint resulted in most local and many national newspapers becoming so brittle in the course of the next forty years that there can now be few complete files of such news-papers in the country. The mid-twenties saw a marked improve-ment in the lasting quality of newsprint with the reduction of the mechanical wood content and the production of one or two of the national newspapers in editions printed on rag paper, but the improvement was short-lived, and the Second World War once again produced a sharp deterioration in the quality of newsprint. From this deterioration newsprint is only now making some recovery, but there seems little likelihood that apart from special rag paper editions such as the Royal edition of *The Times* and the superior paper of such newspapers as the *Manchester Guardian* few are likely to last for a hundred years or even for fifty years if they receive a conventional binding, however detailed, however careful and however expensive it may be.

Newspapers provide an unrivalled source of basic historical information, and it is essential that the most careful consideration should be given to the preservation of this class of material and to its future use. Whatever processes are used the preservation of newspapers is going to be expensive, and it may well be that the first requirement is that a careful allocation of the responsibility for the filing and preservation or recording of newspapers should first be carried out on a national and subsequently on a regional basis. It is, for example, interesting to note from the *London union list of periodicals* that in the London area there are thirty-two bound files of *The Times* in varying degrees of completeness, but all of them being currently maintained. There is only one file of the *Manchester Guardian* and that covers a period of two years.

There are, it seems, three methods of preserving newspaper record. The first and probably the most satisfactory is by micro-filming the complete file and all subsequent issues. Kodak have already carried out the task of preserving *The Times* in this way. In addition a number of libraries have made arrangements for their file of small local newspapers to be micro-filmed, but the larger authorities are likely to find the cost of such a project is prohibitive unless it is heavily subsidized. The problem is not insuperable, however, and the Canadian Library Association with the aid of a capital grant of 15,000 dollars from the Rockefeller Foundation have filmed files of sixty-eight both early and current Canadian newspapers. This aspect of the problem hardly falls within the scope of this book, and with the hope that either the British Museum or the Library Association will at least equal the efforts of the Canadian Library Association we must turn to the second method which is the preservation and sealing off of the individual page.

It may be that certain newspapers will never be in sufficient national demand to justify micro-filming, but it may also happen that such newspapers are of considerable local or regional interest. It seems likely that a costly but reasonably efficient method of preserving such newspapers is to seal off each individual sheet with a film and so prevent the absorption of deleterious chemicals from the atmosphere, and at the same time give the body of the paper a little added strength. The most satisfactory method is probably that adopted for the preservation of the National Archives of the United States of America and described in some detail in Chapter Fourteen on recent developments. By this method a thin film of cellulose acetate is laminated to the paper under pressure and a fairly low heat. Although the cheapest method it is nevertheless quite expensive, costing approximately one shilling for a double-sided page, and the increase in size for a bound volume would be just under an inch for the average quarterly volume consisting of, say, twelve pages to the daily issue. That it would effectively preserve newsprint cannot be doubted if the decision of the Archivist of the U.S.A. and the opinion of the U.S. Bureau of Standards are to be accepted. A third and similar method is that whereby a matt and fairly transparent plastic film is fastened by means of an adhesive to the printed surface. It is a process which has largely been used for the preservation and strengthening of the thin paper used in directories submitted to a good deal of hard wear, and has not, as far as is known, been successfully applied to the long-term preservation of newsprint.

But the majority of librarians are not likely to be persuaded to either micro-film their local newspapers or to case each sheet in cellulose acetate and their principal concern is to ensure that files of newspapers are bound as effectively as possible within the normal conventions of bookbinding. Such librarians must, it seems, face the fact that there are two clear categories of binding for newspapers, just as there are two clear categories of binding in dealing with books from the Reference Library, and these are the binding for immediate and contemporary use and the binding for long-term preservation. In the case of newspapers the obvious solution usually is to bind two quite distinct files for these two quite distinct purposes as there seems to be little point in binding a half-year's newspapers for long-term preservation if, as so often happens, they are going to be pulled to pieces in the next ten years by contemporary use.

Assuming that it is possible to bind newspapers in duplicate in this way, we should give consideration to the most effective method of binding newspapers for long-term preservation. It is essential that no copies of newspapers that are to be used for permanent binding should be allowed to pass into the hands of readers, and they should be carefully stored without folding after they have been examined to see that they are complete and well printed throughout. What is wanted is a volume preferably not more than two inches and certainly not more than three inches thick and the actual binding should consist of a flexible sewing in linen all-along on to six linen tapes with adequate slips for well-made split boards made from millboard. The covering material should consist of an oil- and water-resistant double-warp buckram of not less than 110 threads per square inch, and the endpapers should be of an adequate weight and well folded and reinforced. The American Library Association's minimum specification for Class A library binding, which is given in Appendix II, gives a reasonably detailed and fairly satisfactory specification for this class of work. A binding similar to that produced by the reputable commercial library binders for the librarian who does not ask for leather is what is called for, but in addition a slip case should be provided. Such a slip case should be well fitting and should be equipped in the majority of cases with a front opening flap carrying the title and period—as on the back of the actual volume—and a heavily reinforced head and tail edge. The material used should be of similar quality to that used for the actual volume. The purpose of such a slip case is to protect the volume of newspapers; to reduce the damage by sunlight and to restrict quite substantially but not to eliminate the circulation of air and the dust and sulphur dioxide that goes with the air. The reinforced head and tail ends in the slip case serve to provide a stand for any subsequent volumes laid on top of the slip case, and by using the flap it is possible to leave the slip case on the shelf and so reduce shelf wear.

Such a file is fairly expensive to maintain, but if it is to serve its proper purpose it will inevitably require a file for common use so that the bound file remains in its slip case until the file for current use has either worn out or until the demand is largely that inspired by academic research. This current demand is often very considerable, and a file of newspapers can be reduced to a soiled and tattered mess in meeting it. It is a demand which usually dies in four or five years, and if duplicate sets of newspapers in demand are cheaply bound it will serve to protect the permanent files.

For this cheaper binding unsewn binding could certainly be used, and this with a tight cloth back and cloth-covered boards cut flush give a remarkably cheap and serviceable binding, costing approximately a fifth to a quarter of the conventional binding if a lettered label is used in preference to the conventional gold finished lettering.

PERIODICALS

A conventional commercial library binding for a periodical in a good quality niger morocco and cloth sides is a fairly expensive item, costing usually between twenty and thirty shillings a volume. Given such a binding and reasonably careful use, it seems likely that a volume of periodicals will last reasonably well if the conditions of storage are satisfactory, but the present practice would seem to be often related to the requirements of the previous century, both in the periodicals bound and in the method of binding them. As with newspapers, there is a real need for national, regional and, in some cases, local co-operation in order to ensure that unnecessary duplication is avoided and that coverage is effective. Given such co-operation it would seem to be desirable to divide periodicals into three groups:—first, those periodicals that are of some intellectual standing and that are likely to be of permanent value; second, those that are likely to be the subject of a considerable contemporary demand, and lastly, those that do not appear to be likely to be in considerable demand but for which an occasional demand exists and which may be kept for a limited number of years. It will readily be seen that such categories will vary in range according to the size, type and location of the library, and it may well be that Manchester, for example, would place the *Pottery Gazette* in the third category and the *Journal of the Textile Institute* in the first category, whereas Stoke-on-Trent may quite reasonably reverse the procedure. Nevertheless it may help if it is stated that normally *Mind* or *Nature* might go in the first category, *New Statesman and Nation* might go in the second category, and *Investor's Chronicle* might go in the third category.

It is difficult to give a detailed specification for any category of periodical binding, and certainly in the first category it will often happen that special considerations of paper, format and layout will make any such specification little other than a general guide, but a volume that is sewn all along with linen thread on to at least four linen tapes and which incorporates first-grade materials throughout, including, for example, a double-warp buckram treated to make it stain-resistant and having at least 110 threads per square inch, should serve admirably. A general basis for such a specification is offered by the American Library Association's minimum specification for Class A library binding published as an appendix to this work.

The paper used for periodicals bound in this way is usually superior to newsprint, and the bound volume is not subject to the strain of the heavier newspaper volume, with the result that it should not generally be necessary to fit well-made slip cases for such works, but where atmospheric conditions are not particularly satisfactory there is something to be said for protecting the bound volume of poorer paper in this way.

The second category of periodicals is required to face a fairly considerable amount of use in the immediate future, and what is wanted is a strong and reasonably inexpensive binding of the type now usually carried out by the commercial library binder and consisting of a quarter binding of niger sewn either all along or oversewn by hand in reasonably sized sections.

The third category is a storage binding which is designed to be inexpensive and merely provides storage facilities superior to the loose filing of periodicals. Here again unsewn binding can serve admirably with a tight cloth back, uncovered boards cut flush and a titling label—the cost of such a binding is trifling compared with that of the other two categories.

In preparing and organizing this material prior to its being bound, it is necessary to maintain a periodical binding record file with a card for each periodical that is bound and this card should state the title, frequency of publication, frequency of binding, frequency of publication of index, when this is due, source of index, binder, class of binding, colour, lettering instructions, whether advertising material and covers are to be included, and any special instructions.

On the reverse of the card are details of date covered by each volume, volume number or numbers, date of dispatch, special instructions, date of return.

A well-planned organization for this class of work will result in the saving of both money and time, and in neatly uniform volumes of complete runs.

The normal practice for periodicals is to lay down the pattern for the first volume to be bound, and then either send a rubbing of the standard volume when subsequent volumes are dispatched or alternatively a pattern volume is sent. The conventional practice in lettering the spine is to give the title in the upper part of the back, and then state the volume number in the centre of the back. This is followed by the dates covered by the volume, and at the bottom appears the classification number.

Our colleagues in the U.S.A. have overcome their rugged individualism to the extent of formulating a code of standardized lettering for magazine binding, and it seems reasonable that a similar code should be drawn up in this country for general guidance either by the Library Association or by the British Standards Institution.

PAMPHLETS

A pamphlet is usually taken to be a single section work in paper covers, but a more general interpretation would seem to be any paper-covered work of less than five sections. For our purposes the second of these two definitions will be accepted, and again it is necessary in considering how best to preserve such material to classify according to value and to use.

It is possible by padding out a pamphlet with additional sections of blank paper to give it the binding and protection afforded by the conventional bookbinding, but such a practice is hardly necessary except for the bibliographical rarity. The majority of those pamphlets which are considered to be worthy of permanent preservation can be sewn and pasted into pamphlet cases. This process necessitates guarding the spine of the pamphlet with two sheets of white cover paper and a strip of white linen, all of which are then sewn together in the conventional way through the fold of the single section. The case is made quite separately, usually in quarter cloth, and the pamphlet is then placed in the case and the endpapers and reinforcements are pasted down. A superior type of case with quarter leather and good cloth sides is occasionally used, but this would seem to be a rather heavy and extravagant use of materials under normal circumstances.

Recent developments in the making and application of transparent films would seem to be of value in preserving this rather difficult class of material, particularly where the cover of the pamphlet is printed on one side only and can be mounted on light board and then covered with polythene or cellulose acetate. The most conventional, the cheapest, and apart from binding pamphlets together in miscellaneous volumes, quite the least efficient is to keep pamphlets grouped in pamphlet boxes. These boxes with hinged tops or with top and bottom fitting into each other like a telescope are usually cloth covered, fairly well made and supplied by the library suppliers. They have their uses for the fugitive material which is rarely referred to, but for pamphlets and similar material which are fairly frequently referred to and which can be grouped by subject interest—the smaller trade catalogues for example—there is a good deal to be said for the stiff-backed case carrying either wires or threads. Each pair of wires or threads is used to carry a pamphlet, and such a case of four inches thick can normally carry up to fifty items, any of which can be quickly consulted and easily withdrawn and replaced.

Well-made boxes can serve many useful purposes, particularly in a large reference library where they are used for the filing of periodicals, for the protection of pamphlets and other fugitive material, for the filing of illustrations and for the protection of rare books in fine bindings. The most widely known variety of these boxes is called the Solander Book Box (after its inventor of the British Museum), who introduced the case for the protection and preservation of books in 1773. In spite of a good deal of confusion in the various American books on this matter, there is little doubt that the Solander case actually consists of a carefully made, nicely fitting lidded box with the front cover hinged at the spine and closing to form an overlapping joint and head, tail and fore-edge. The case is usually finished in cloth or leather and both lettered and ornamented. Its value can be demonstrated by an examination of the condition of those books which have been protected in this way for more than a century, and it is certainly true that in the disastrous floods which severely damaged the library at the Tate Gallery many of the books were subsequently discovered floating in their Solander cases but quite undamaged.

A more usual type of book box is the telescope type, which is made in two parts and fits together by means of a deep collar on the bottom part of the box over which the top part of the box can slide.

For fine books it is the practice to give them the protection of either a slip case or a chemise. The slip case or thumb case is usually tailored to the individual book and consists of a five-sided, limp cloth-covered case which when made correctly should fit snugly so that the case does not slip off easily nor should it be so tight that it must be pulled off. Normally the back of the book is

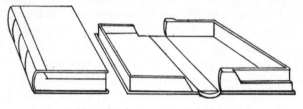

THE SOLANDER BOOK BOX

left uncovered, but there are many variations on the basic pattern and sometimes a flap is provided on the sixth side in order to protect the back of the book. Occasionally the edges are stiffened in order to give additional protection.

The chemise is a loose protective covering for a fine binding or a rare book, either as an alternative to or in addition to the Solander case. This cover is usually covered with leather, occasionally in cloth and more rarely in green baize. It is made so that it has an overlap with a fold-over flap for the front and back boards.

MUSIC

The binding and preservation of music is now carried out according to a sound and conventional pattern by most commercial library binders. The individual work is usually bound in full cloth and lettered on the spine. A number of libraries use differently coloured cloths to distinguish between the various broad classes of music, and all piano works are, for example, bound in red, all orchestral works in green, all chamber music in blue and all vocal scores in brown.

If the complementary parts of a score can reasonably be given a limp binding and fitted into a pocket at the back of the main part which is given a conventional stiff binding, it would seem to be the most efficient way of dealing with this rather intractable material. If there are more parts than will conveniently allow this to be done they should either be bound separately or each part should be given a limp binding and fitted into a large slip case with a stiff back carrying the lettering.

Sheet music is usually either bound up into a composite volume —an unnecessarily wasteful and extravagant practice—or filed in a vertical file and then issued in a slightly modified manilla folder with a pocket inside the front flap. A most interesting and useful development has been the cheap and successful lamination of sheet music with a transparent film, and this process is described more fully under the chapter on recent developments.

MAPS

The most usual way of strengthening maps is to mount them either complete or in sections on linen or fine strong muslin. The linen is first stretched and pinned down before it is moistened in order to overcome the difficulty of dealing with shrinkage during the actual mounting process. The linen is then cut to size with a reasonable overlap all round and pinned down on a drawing-board. If the map is to be mounted in sections then the linen is marked up with the placings of the individual sections. The map is then pasted and all surplus paste removed before it is pressed down on the reinforcing linen and left to dry under pressure. When it is dry the pins are released and the edges trimmed.

A cheap and fairly effective method of protecting maps which are only subject to occasional use is by means of edge binding. The material used can be either paper or cloth, usually half an inch wide. The most satisfactory would appear to be a self-adhesive cotton tape supplied in reels suitable for the edge binder. This is a simple, inexpensive machine manufactured by a well-known firm of office machinery manufacturers and is quite simple to operate. The protection of the map by lamination with a cellulose acetate film is described in the chapter on recent developments.

MANUSCRIPTS AND SIMILAR MATERIAL

The method originally used in the Public Record Office and outlined by Sir Hilary Jenkinson in his book *A Manual of Archive Administration* is now widely used by archivists and librarians. The process consists of fastening a fine silk net over the surface of the manuscript or print by means of a carefully prepared chemical-free paste made from corn flour. The finished work is nicely strengthened by a process which does little to reduce the legibility of the surface treated and which is accepted as appropriate in our most important depositories. Nevertheless we should not overlook the claims of more modern material and in America the use of cellulose acetate for this same purpose has the patronage of the Archivist of the U.S.A. and has been tested by the National Bureau of Standards in that country. This process is also considered in the chapter on recent developments.

CHAPTER ELEVEN

The repair and care of books and bookbindings

SUCH A topic could embrace the whole art of bookbinding, but the care and repair of books is used here to mean those processes which are not essentially a part of bookbinding but which are often carried out by the bookbinder in his work of restoring and preserving a book. The line between the two is rather vague, but, for example, it will be found that guarding—an essential part of bookbinding—is described in the chapter on forwarding by hand, but the repair and restoration of torn or stained pages falls into this chapter.

Probably the commonest type of book repair is to the torn page. If the tear consists of a missing corner the first step is to find a matching piece of paper, and this can often be taken from a spare fly-leaf, but many bookbinders keep a sizeable store of old end-papers for just this purpose. The torn corner is pared with an exceedingly sharp knife so that the thickness of the paper is tapered down and the replacement paper is also pared. The two edges are lightly pasted and then joined together and kept under pressure between sheets of waxed paper. With a little practice an almost invisible joint can be made.

The more usual tear in the page which is so often repaired by the enthusiastic assistant armed with a paste pot and the conviction that all that is needed is a good strip of paste brushed on with vigour is usually repaired in the conventional book by a narrow strip of transparent paper tape pasted down over the tear, but with a little patience, even less paste, and a small supply of soft tissue paper it is possible to give a torn page an almost invisible repair and reinforcement. It will be seen that the tear always has an overlap—sometimes this overlap moves from one side of the paper to the other, but it should be lightly and carefully pasted and then tissue should be firmly pressed over the tear back and front and further pressure applied through a sandwich of wax paper.

A small amount of paste will be squeezed out of the tear and adhere to the tissue, and when the paste is dry it will be found that the tissue paper can be pulled away, leaving an almost invisible reinforcement to the joined edges of the paper.

Occasionally it is necessary to give a substantial reinforcement to a badly crumpled or worn page, and the method used by the Public Record Office and known in the U.S.A. as *crepeline* is possibly the safest and most satisfactory. It consists of pasting a fine silk gauze to both sides of the paper, and this network gives an almost invisible reinforcement of considerable strength. The method by which this process is carried out is quite straightforward, but as it is not generally known nor described in print the following outline may be of value. The material to be reinforced is laid out on a clean smooth surface, such as glass or Formica, and then well damped so that it is fully stretched. Whilst the paper is still damp the silk gauze is laid over and a thin coating carefully prepared. Dextrine paste is brushed on, working from the centre outwards. It is only in this way that a smooth surface can be achieved. A description of the use of cellulose acetate for this work is dealt with in the chapter on recent developments.

In craft binding it is occasionally necessary to wash the leaves of old books in order to restore their appearance and so increase their legibility, and it is also frequently carried out after the removal of stains. Done well, this process can effect the most startling improvements in the appearance of a book. Done carelessly, it can leave a residue of active chemicals which will rot the treated pages in a surprisingly short time. It is an expensive and time-consuming process which involves placing the leaves in a bath of hot water with a little alum added, and their being left to soak for some hours. The careful handling of the wet leaves, their subsequent resizing and their complete drying is the simplest and the safest process, but occasionally a book which is stained will require some stronger chemical action to bring out the stains. There are few stains which cannot be fairly effectively removed, but as this usually necessitates a bleach, it is a process that requires careful control and a fair amount of experience if the paper is not to be damaged. The conventional method is to use baths of permanganate of potash followed by diluted sulphurous acid and then by hyposulphate of soda as a neutralizer. The process is completed with two or three hours' washing in running water and the paper is then toned to match the original colour before being resized.

The process of sizing or resizing paper is not only used for the leaves which have been cleaned and washed; it can also be used profitably to restore the strength and surface of old paper which has become soft with age or, as happens more frequently, because it has been exposed to moisture or a damp atmosphere.

The pages to be sized are cleaned with a soft rubber or with a ball of moistened bread as otherwise the size will permanently seal in any marks on the paper.

The size bath consists of a warm, weak solution of gelatine, and the washed or weakened pages are passed through fairly quickly before they are squeezed between blotting-paper and then hung to dry on cords.

The most acute problem confronting many librarians is the question of the repair, restoration, recasing or rebinding of old books in the reference library. There are few libraries without a fairly sizeable heritage of books which are gently mouldering on the shelves. Many such books are not a century old, others are only slightly weakened after three centuries of wear. The librarian's first duty is to know how to arrest such decay and this is dealt with later in the section on the care of books, but the damage has often been done and a book taken from the shelf will result in a red, rusty stain on hands and clothes and a pair of boards separated from the book. Is the book to be re-bound or restored? Generally speaking, the purpose of restoring a binding is to save something which has an artistic or historic value. It would be essential to restore if at all possible an Eliot and Chapman binding or a Samuel Mearne binding, and it would be equally desirable to restore an English blind stamped binding of the sixteenth century. It is quite ridiculous to restore a nineteenth-century binding in red calf—it is almost as ridiculous to restore an eighteenth-century binding unless the binding or book has some particular characteristics which justify an attempt at complete preservation, as it must be emphasized that the restoration of a binding is an expensive business and by its nature it is usually more expensive and less efficient than rebinding a book.

Let us assume that it has been decided that a binding shall be restored and that the restoration will call for rebacking, the strengthening or replacement of the attachment between boards and spine, the building up of the boards at their edges and corners, the replacement of damaged or worn leather, and the replacement of all the original leather on top of the new, wherever this is possible. Such a restoration calls for a high degree of skill and a knowledge of early craftsmanship on the part of the book-binder, and some knowledge of the processes that are to be carried out by the librarian or individual who commissions the work.

The first step is to take a rubbing of the spine so that a pattern exists to enable the spine to be accurately reconstructed. Then the leather is taken from the spine, and as in the majority of cases the book will not be a hollow back this is a difficult task if the spine is to be worth restoring after removal. Leather, if it is not too decayed, can usually be lifted off with a sharp knife by splitting the leather and leaving a layer behind, but it is more often necessary to cut off a panel at a time, and even so with larger books it is usually advisable to strengthen the spine by first pasting over it a web of mull or fine silk.

With the spine clear and the surplus leather scraped away the sewing should be tested. Although many sixteenth- and seventeenth-century books are still remarkably strong in the sewing, if there is looseness or break in the sewing the book should be pulled and resewn on cords.

It will often be found that if the sewing is intact in books bound before the nineteenth century the cords are also strong and provide an effective hinge for the boards, but again if there is any appreciable wear it will be worth cutting the boards from the book and renewing the cords.

The endpapers should be lifted, given a reinforcing linen tape at the back and pasted down again if they bear any book plates or manuscript notes. Otherwise the opportunity should be taken to replace them with a carefully folded and reinforced endpaper, details of which are given in the chapter on bookbinding by hand—forwarding.

The spine should then be reglued and carefully rounded and rebacked. Such a procedure will usually throw the boards out of true, but these can subsequently be trimmed down at the spine edge so that they fit nicely. The make-up of the original head-bands can usually be traced at the "tie down" and a reasonable copy can be produced—it is worth the trouble if tiresome anachronisms are to be avoided.

The boards should now be made good, and the usual method of repairing corners is by lifting the leather of the old corners and then reinforcing underneath with new matching leather. Often the corners are knocked or badly worn and a new corner is then built up from a compound of paste and fine board filings. The worn leather at the edges of the boards is lifted away from its separated turn-in which is also removed and a new ribbon of matching leather is fitted.

Preparing the boards for the fitting of the new spinal leather calls for precise handling of tools and an accurate preparation of matching leather. The old covering leather is lifted for a depth of an inch or so from the spine edge and a narrow strip trimmed off and fastened down at the spine edge so that the edge of the old cover does not project unduly above the new reinforcing leather fastened down below it. This new leather needs to be cut with a generous allowance for a turn-in at head and tail, and the main edges should be carefully chamfered down so that they will fit neatly under the thinned edges of the old leather on the covers.

The back of the old leather from the spine is scraped clean and thinned so that it will lie evenly on the newly covered spine, and the new leather is then roughened up to receive the freshly pasted leather of the old spine. The book is then bandaged so that a good joint is effected, and when dried the spine is carefully rubbed smooth and the work of restoration should be complete.

It may be that the finished work will be improved by giving the old leather a toning-up, either by means of a paste wash or by cleaning with ether soap, but a thin solution of polyvinyl acetate which has been carefully brushed on is also extremely effective.

In handling this type of work the librarian and the bookbinder should be on their guard so that they may avoid the anachronism of the seventeenth-century book with gilded edges or the sixteenth-century book with a French joint. It is, of course, equally absurd to pursue the restoration to the point of feeble forgery or slavish imitation, and if the result gives us a sound and serviceable book which displays the original binding to its full advantage we will have achieved a satisfactory restoration.

As Dr. Plenderleith of the British Museum has shown by his careful and painstaking research, it is possible to prolong the life of leather bindings very considerably by appropriate treatment, either by ensuring that the leather used in the first place is PIRA tested or by treating the binding with a solution incorporating potassium lactate. This treatment advocated by Dr. Plenderleith in his pamphlet also recommends the use of a leather dressing, but it seems doubtful whether this dressing serves any purpose other than to give a superficial and quite temporary gloss to the leather.

Subsequently Unwin and Middleton in the *Museums Journal* advocated the use of a leather preservative based on Dr. Plenderleith's formula, but combining potassium lactate, leather dressing and polyvinyl acetate in one preparation. This would appear to be satisfactory, but it is rather difficult of application and does not appear to show that degree of penetration which is required if the potassium lactate is to do its work properly. It is recommended that a dressing of potassium lactate followed by a coating of polyvinyl acetate suspended in a solution of toluol should be used as in this way the leather will be rendered resistant to the chemical action of sulphur dioxide by the presence of potassium lactate, and this resistance will be reinforced by a protective film of polyvinyl acetate on top of the leather. Such treatment is not costly in either material or time, and librarians with any number of rarely used leather-bound books would be well advised to ensure that they are protected in this way if they wish to avoid the far heavier expense of restoration and binding.

Rare bindings can and should be treated with the potassium lactate solution, but there is also a great deal to be said for the making of special covers for such books. The Solander box may be used, but a loosely fitting baize cover protects the binding without any danger of scratching it and so affords a cheap and effective protection.

Without any doubt the most harmful influence on bindings, after careless handling by readers and staff, is the deterioration caused by atmospheric pollution, and in particular by sulphur dioxide. Although the problem is not quite as acute as it was in the days of gaslighting, it is nevertheless a real source of deterioration in our larger cities, and here the treatment already outlined is advocated for all libraries which are not provided with efficient air-cleaning plant.

The Royal Society of Arts in their reports on leather for bookbinding were firmly of the opinion that strong light and hot air had a most harmful influence on leather bindings, and this opinion will be readily confirmed by anybody who has examined leather-bound books which have been exposed to sunlight for a year or two, as not only does the leather crumble at the touch but the paper of the book itself will usually be found to have become brittle. The obvious solution is not to shelve valuable books so that they are exposed to sunlight, but where this is not possible blinds should be fitted.

In this country the problem of excessive atmospheric dryness is not likely to cause the librarian much trouble, but in many other countries the damage done to books and bookbindings by dry heat is very considerable. The demand for a high winter temperature indoors often leads to lack of humidity which can quickly dry out leather, book construction materials and the paper of any book. The answer is an effective air-conditioning plant, but where this is not available a check can be kept on the relative humidity by means of an hygrometer and appropriate action taken by exposing water surfaces near the actual heating surfaces.

Dampness with the accompanying mould and mildew is a far more usual problem for British librarians, and this is usually brought about by a combination of dampness and inadequate circulation. The dampness is usually caused by the books coming in contact with a defective wall or floor, but it is possible for books to be damaged by damp if there is inadequate circulation of air. The remedy is fairly obvious, namely, to keep the books away from walls and floors as a matter of general routine; to ensure that such walls and floors are in any case dry, and finally all rooms used for book storage should be well ventilated. The damage caused by mould and mildew is often irreparable as it breaks down the adhesive, softens the leather and causes a disintegration of the paper. If the damage is not too far advanced it is possible to brush away the mould and wipe the surface clean with surgical alcohol, finishing off with a dressing of thymol in order to sterilize it.

The effect of dust on books is not as harmful as is usually imagined, and more harm is often done by the well-intentioned cleaner who gives the dusty book a buffeting and then wipes it or the shelf down with a damp rag to catch the dust. All books are better for an occasional dusting—the frequency varying with the situation and the age of the library—the only satisfactory procedure is for an intelligent cleaner to be trained in this work. The books are to be handled gently and cleaned with a specially equipped vacuum cleaner and soft clean rags. The shelves are to be cleared and wiped over with an old polish rag followed by a clean polishing rag. The vacuum cleaner should not be a small machine carried by hand, but a fairly powerful cylindrical type fitted in a sound-insulated case and equipped with small brushes attached to a tube.

If this work is carried out every year—and this seems to be a reasonable interval—there is a good deal to be said in favour of a bookbinder following close behind the cleaner checking up which books require dressing, repair, restoration and binding.

Of the many insects that attack books and bookbindings the so-called bookworm is the most troublesome. In fact the bookworm is almost invariably the common furniture beetle—*Anobium punctatum*—and it is the most troublesome because it probably does the greatest amount of damage to books in this country and because it exercises such discrimination in only choosing the older books for its activities. The reason for this, it is presumed, is the modern practice of using alum in paste and latex in glue. It is certainly unwise to assume that the larvae of *A. punctatum* are not at work in any collection of old books as these creatures can and do bore through cupboards and shelves. In fact, the usual evidence that this pest is at work is the little piles of wood or leather ejected from the hole produced by the bookworm. Where such a hole is detected the book affected should be isolated immediately and the paper inspected. If the larvae is found it should be destroyed. If the paper has not been attacked it should be protected by the insertion of metal plates inside the boards, and the holes in the boards should be treated with a preparation containing orthodichlorobenzene, or the whole book should be placed in an inverted jar with a little ethylene oxide. The cupboard or shelf from which the infected book was taken should be carefully examined as should all neighbouring books and immediate treatment given to any damage. It is as well to disinfect the cupboard with a sprinkling of D.D.T.

Cockroaches are sometimes a nuisance in that they occasionally attack and foul the filler in the book cloth. A further most objectionable characteristic is that they give off a musty smell which is found in old buildings that are not as well lit or as well ventilated as they should be. The remedy is not easy to find—improved ventilation, plenty of sunshine, the introduction of polished rather than washed floors will all help, but special disinfectants such as gammexane or D.D.T. are called for. Incidentally, the cockroach comes out in the dark, and another disinfectant consisting of 1 part of pyrethrum to 3 parts of sodium chloride could be laid down on a liberal scale at regular intervals until the pest is cleared. A more detailed study of the pests that attack books and effective methods for the protection of both old and new books against such attacks is given in an excellent paper in *Journal of Documentation*, vol. 9, no. 3, for September 1953.

The life of a book may be shortened by any or all of these influences, but the most vital influence is the treatment the book receives by the staff who handle and the readers who use it. If the book is pulled off a shelf that carries too many books by means of the head of the spine it will soon be without both boards and spine. If the book is not returned to the shelf carefully the contents of the book can easily be damaged. If the book is dropped the sewing is most likely to be broken, and certainly the boards are likely to be crumpled. All books should be handled with care; old books should be handled with respect.

CHAPTER TWELVE

Administration. Expenditure on bookbinding. Present methods of controlling expenditure, etc.

IN THE fourth edition of *Public libraries* dated 1891, Greenwood has a page and a half devoted to bookbinding in which he states: "A book bound in half pigskin according to the following specification will stand almost anything short of use as a firebrick." Then follows the specification, including "if thought necessary vellum corners". The cost of such a binding for a novel was 1*s*. 4*d*.! His principal concern was, however, not with the considerable advantage which came from using pigskin but rather with the need for a careful consideration of when to bind a book. "It is much cheaper in the end", he writes, "and more judicious to take the wear out of the original binding even though it be only paper boards, as there is always the risk of books never being in demand, and the cost of binding is then thrown away." To reinforce his point he went on: "A cloth copy of *East Lynne* can be bought in London for 2*s*. 4*d*. With constant use, and no ill-treatment it will remain in fair condition for twelve or eighteen months. It can then be re-bound in half pigskin for another 1*s*. 4*d*. and will probably last another two years, at the end of which time it will be very dirty."

In his day Mr. Greenwood served the cause of public libraries well. His advice was usually sound and eminently practical. Today no librarian would consider his advice on bookbinding materials realistic, but it cannot be doubted that many librarians would profit from a more careful consideration of what books to bind and how to bind them most efficiently. Can it also be that many librarians today are circulating copies of contemporary novels until they are very dirty?

An attempt to make some statistical evaluation of the expenditure on bookbinding by the public libraries of Great Britain and Northern Ireland is clearly necessary if consideration is to be given to the administration of bookbinding with a view to formulating some general policy in this matter.

If 1954–55 is compared with 1952–53—the years for which accurate and fairly detailed figures are available—it will be found that in 1952–53 the total expenditure by public libraries on books and binding combined was £3,692,000, and of this 22·3 per cent or £823,000 was spent on binding. In 1954–55 the total expenditure on books and binding combined was £4,000,000, and of this 20·5 per cent or £820,000 was spent on binding. Stated another way, in 1952–53 for every £1 spent on books 5s. 9d. was spent on binding, and in 1954–55 for every £1 spent on books 5s. 1d. was spent on binding.

It will be recognized that these figures for binding are to be regarded as approximations of average figures. The figures for binding expenditure do not presumably include the full cost of library binderies, nor do they include the additional cost of books already bound in library editions. That 5s. 9d. for 1952–53 and 5s. 1d. for 1954–55 are average figures will be established when it is pointed out that in 1952–53 Birmingham spent 8s. 11d. on binding for every £1 spent on books, whereas Blackpool spent 4s. and Bolton 2s. 4d. In 1954–55—as will be seen from the following tables—Birmingham spent 8s. 8d., whereas Blackpool spent 3s. 3d. and Bolton 2s. 3d. In the counties the figures show just as wide a variation—in 1952–53 Cornwall spent 9s. 4d. on binding for every £1 spent on books, Buckingham spent 4s. 11d., Devon 10s. 8d. and Durham 5s. 2d. For 1954–55 the corresponding figures are Cornwall 7s. 10d., Buckingham 3s. 10d., Devon 9s. 1d. and Durham 5s. 8d.

The table overleaf gives a fairly representative sample of the larger public library authorities. The first three columns of figures are doubtless open to special interpretation in a number of cases. They may, for example, include special provision under book expenditure for the stocking of new libraries, and it could be argued that the expenditure on bookbinding should be related to the book expenditure in earlier years, but accepting all reasonable doubts the figures give us a comparatively clear picture of the situation.

The fifth column is an interpretation of columns two and three,

AN ANALYSIS OF BOOKS AND BOOKBINDING EXPENDITURE IN 1954–55 IN A NUMBER OF PUBLIC LIBRARY AUTHORITIES SERVING POPULATIONS IN EXCESS OF 100,000

1	2	3	4	5	6
Authority	Home reading issues	Expenditure on books	Expenditure on binding	Expenditure on binding for every £1 spent on books	Issues per volume at 10s. per volume
				s. d.	
Battersea	987,820	9,276	2,250	4 10	53
Birmingham	6,038,545	42,858	18,559	8 8	70
Blackburn	709,394	4,646	849	3 8	76
Blackpool	1,812,876	10,766	1,756	3 3	84
Bolton	1,407,747	9,665	1,080	2 3	73
Bournemouth	2,197,610	14,143	3,207	4 6	77
Bradford	2,281,803	17,938	3,569	4 0	64
Bristol	3,152,174	38,227	8,967	4 8	41
Camberwell	1,509,169	16,732	3,506	4 2	45
Cardiff	2,420,429	15,708	5,935	7 7	77
Coventry	2,143,009	12,902	3,535	5 6	83
Croydon	1,900,018	12,466	6,348	10 2	76
Dagenham	901,443	10,586	4,670	8 10	43
Derby	1,272,108	7,075	2,424	6 10	90
Ealing	1,844,276	18,344	3,052	3 4	50
East Ham	905,672	6,984	1,486	4 3	65
Edmonton	509,848	4,803	1,650	6 10	53
Enfield	564,085	5,178	1,728	6 8	55
Fulham	887,716	10,454	2,990	5 9	42
Bedfordshire	1,018,637	9,238	2,805	6 1	55
Buckingham	2,039,938	21,303	3,920	3 8	48
Cheshire	2,063,164	18,203	5,021	5 6	57
Cornwall	1,659,825	9,462	3,696	7 10	88
Devonshire	3,426,403	19,110	8,714	9 1	90
Dorsetshire	1,213,306	7,008	2,500	7 1	87
Durham	5,364,938	43,948	12,514	5 8	61
Essex	6,707,989	74,824	16,117	4 4	44
Gloucestershire	1,695,485	14,811	2,693	3 8	57

and the figures would seem to indicate a variation which points to an inconsistency of approach to the problem of bookbinding. It would be naïve to expect the same level of bookbinding expenditure in an urban authority such as, for example, Bournemouth, as is found in a large industrial centre such as, for example, Birmingham with its large regional responsibilities. Nevertheless it would be true to say that the only conclusion that can be reached at this stage is to state that there is little consistency between similar authorities in this matter.

Column number six requires some fairly detailed explanation. The amount of binding for the home reading libraries is related to the use made of these libraries, and to enable some comparison to be made it has been assumed that the book expenditure is devoted entirely to books for the home reading libraries. Obviously then the allowance for book expenditure in relation to home reading issues is too large, and to those authorities with disproportionately large reference departments it is much too large. If, to offset this, and in order to reach some comparable figures, it is assumed that all new books added to the home reading libraries cost 10s. per volume the total estimated number of books acquired can be arrived at. Assuming that the number of books acquired is fairly constant over the previous five years the figure of issues per volume would give a reasonable figure, but an examination of previous years show, as might be expected, that the total number of books acquired has increased. It can thus be stated that the figure in column six is probably an understatement of the issues per volume for each authority.

In spite of all these suppositions column six serves then to support the view that in general those libraries securing a high average issue per volume spend more on bookbinding, but even allowing for this it can also be stated that bearing in mind the large number of books which are out of date or worn out before they have reached the average issue life there are a large number of authorities making excessive demands from the books they buy.

Against this general statistical background it should be possible to consider the need for a general bookbinding policy. In formulating such a policy our colleagues in the United States have the advantage of us in that they have a Library Binding Institute. This institute is a liaison between the American Library Association and the commercial library binders. Its moving spirit for many years was the late Pelham Barr, and it has under continuous review the problems and needs of both librarians and bookbinders. A joint committee of the American Library Association and the Library Binding Institute was created in 1934, and this committee published a minimum specification for Class A library binding, and this specification has been frequently revised so that it can be used with confidence by American librarians in sending their instructions to their bookbinders. This specification deals not only with rebinding books but also with rebinding periodicals and newspapers, and although it is not quite appropriate for British bookbinders it provides an admirable basis for a modified specification, and is therefore published as an appendix to this book, by permission of the Library Binding Institute. This joint committee has also dealt with such matters as a standard lettering system for periodicals and been responsible for the publication of the useful *Library binding manual* in 1951. More important, it has emphasized the importance of policy for bookbinding and encouraged librarians to use the service of bookbinders economically and intelligently. In this country the Library Binders Section of the British Federation of Master Printers and the Library Association have founded a joint committee, but it has rarely met. Whether this is because the binders have no problems and librarians are quite satisfied or whether the binders despair for the librarians, and the librarians are too frustrated to bother, it is hard to say. There seems little doubt that this is a joint committee which could be doing useful work.

The purpose of bookbinding is twofold—it should extend the useful working life of a book and it should ensure that a book is preserved for posterity. In the first category come most of the books bound for the home reading departments and in the second comes a good part of the reference binding. In this first category there are fiction, non-fiction and juvenile books, and without any doubt this is the largest category and one which justifies the closest scrutiny.

How is the binding of fiction controlled in many of our

libraries? Junior assistants take out those books which prevent them from holding a column of books under their chins, and after a cursory examination pick out a few books and put their thumbs in the hinge just to ensure that they really do need binding. They are then dropped on the bottom shelf of the counter and cleared out from time to time to the binding dump. Periodically a consignment is prepared by somebody picking out the appropriate number of books and listing them before sending them to the library binder. Then follows the inevitable correspondence stating that the 500 books have been reduced in some mysterious way to 497, and that the binder has not got book x but has got book y and is it the wish of the librarian that book y be returned? After a week or so there is another flurry of correspondence on the subject of imperfect copies. Finally the books are returned, together with an invoice pricing each book bound by size, and after the books have been counted and checked the book cards are restored and they are returned to the shelves in their fine new covers. The reader picks up the newly bound book, opens it with a crack, and there, far too often are the grubby pages of a book which did too many issues before it was bound and which has cost 4s. to have it re-bound. The reader not knowing all this and merely seeing a book with a crisp new cover concealing far from crisp new pages feels cheated.

On the shelf it takes its place with other re-bound novels of varying ages and in varying stages of wear. The dreary dark brown leather of thirty years ago is now rarely used for fiction, and although Arnold Bennett would no longer refer to those palimpsests of filth as he did in 1909 there are many libraries where the fiction stocks are overworked, and with the advance of more highly coloured dirt-resistant cloths there is a tendency to maintain an outwardly dull but clean fiction stock with deplorably dirty pages.

The problem of non-fiction is even more intractable. It would seem that today many non-fiction books are bound when they should be thrown away. Out-of-date books use up valuable space. Titles which were bought in considerable numbers to meet bestseller demands are bound up because it seems an extravagance to throw away a book which has not completed its full physical life and so these titles appear on the shelves in their twos and threes in library bindings.

Too often the so-called reserve stock becomes a repository of books that were bound when they should have been discarded and so tends to become an elaborate monument to the lack of both courage and discrimination by their librarians. It can be said with a measure of truth that too often the book that is in public demand is worn out and discarded, whereas those for which public demand has ceased are re-bound and stored.

In the reference library the problem of binding is closely related to book stock policy. In those libraries that aspire to rival the British Museum in their completeness all books are bound as required. There would seem to be little discrimination between those books bound for posterity and those books bound to meet contemporary demands, nor would there seem to be any recognition of the need for the careful selection and rejection of books at a time when 18,110 titles are being produced in this country alone each year. The policy controlling the addition and withdrawal of books to reference departments controls the bookbinding policy, and if, as seems likely, too many books are being preserved in too many reference libraries then the policy of binding a large number of books in such departments merely exaggerates this difficulty. The problem can best be exemplified by a consideration of the binding policy for newspapers and periodicals which take a large slice of the binding allocation of many reference libraries. As far as is known no reference library buys and binds all newspapers and periodicals, and the selection of newspapers and periodicals would seem to be more related to the needs of the last century than this. The list of newspapers and periodicals filed and bound is often even more startling in its inconsistencies.

This is the problem briefly stated. It points fairly clearly to the need for more carefully controlled and discriminating binding of books for all departments. In the home reading libraries it is necessary to recognize that the time has passed when bookbinding can be used to perpetuate a dirty book stock. The public will not be satisfied with a social service which offers them soiled well-bound books, and the librarian in either rural area or town who is satisfied with such a service discredits his profession and the community he serves.

But before an answer to the problem of binding for home reading libraries can be found it is necessary to ascertain some basic facts upon which to build, and to do this a survey of fiction in use was carried out in 1954 at a fairly busy home reading library issuing 210,000 volumes of fiction per annum. The book stock was clean and of a fairly high literary standard. Generally speaking, the books were reasonably well cared for, and approximately three-quarters of the books on the shelves had been bound.

On the day of the survey all works of fiction totalling 897 were withdrawn and examined, and the following relevant observations arose out of the survey.

Publishers' cases

(i) The life of a publisher's case is much longer than was anticipated. The average life was 27·8 issues. There is a considerable variation producing this average, ranging from six to fifty-two issues.

(ii) In a crown 8vo it is generally the covering of the spine that goes first followed by the inner joint.

(iii) In a demy 8vo it is usually the inner joint that goes first followed by the spine.

(iv) The books in which the inner joint is reinforced with mull maintain their strength and their shape, but the large number of books which are reinforced at the inner joint with brown paper or a bonded fibre fabric are not so satisfactory. The relative issue values as far as they could be isolated were thirty for mull and twenty for other materials.

(v) The number of unsewn books (3) was not sufficient to draw any conclusions.

(vi) The use of cloth substitutes such as Linson was not as undesirable a development as it was expected to be. Such materials appear to give reasonable service on slimmer books, one of which had been issued forty-nine times.

Re-bound books

(i) The average life of a re-bound book would appear to be about fifty issues.

133

(ii) The use of coloured foil as opposed to gold-leaf is quite satisfactory as far as wearing qualities go.

(iii) The general standard of finishing is high, and books retain their nicely designed lettering throughout their useful life.

(iv) Re-bound books tend to lose their shape after thirty issues as a result of the spine sliding. No completely convincing explanation of this has been offered, but it seems likely that the method of sewing is responsible.

If it is assumed that the cost of the average novel is 10*s*. it will be seen that the cost per issue during the life of such a book is 4*d*. until it is re-bound when the cost becomes 2*d*. per issue, and the actual average cost per issue of the re-bound book is 1*d*. This rather startling comparison in favour of binding is offset to some extent by the preference of the public for new books in their dust jackets and, if these are not available, for clean attractive books in publishers' cases. Certainly a rather heavy price is paid in many libraries for the economy achieved by binding books as the shelves are reduced to a dull monotony.

Recognizing this situation, librarians have given some thought to the possibilities of protecting the most vulnerable parts of a new book and have experimented with various types of reinforcing tapes for the inner joints and a wide variety of transparent films for the dust jacket. These experiments are dealt with in the chapter on recent developments. It would seem likely from a careful examination of the books used in the survey already mentioned above and a study of a large number of books used for experimental purposes that in the average home reading library it would be possible to ensure a life of sixty issues for fiction if the jackets were suitably protected and the inner joints appropriately reinforced. If such a process could be carried out at the cost of 1*s*. per volume it will be seen that the cost per issue is just over 2*d*., and there are the considerable advantages in that each book would be subjected to less wear and the books on the shelf would be cleaner and more attractive. If this procedure were adopted it would result in fewer books being bound and the estimated reduction in the large experimental batch was in the neighbourhood of from 75 to 10 per cent.

But it is necessary to be realistic about such a policy, and there are at present few libraries that allow £1 for every 120 fiction issues. There are, however, many with book funds that are so inadequate that every book must be issued an average of ninety to a hundred times, and under such circumstances the librarian must rebind books on a fairly generous scale, and both he and his authority must accept the fact that a good part of the book stock is dirty.

Reference library binding is a problem which only seriously affects the larger library systems and will receive the briefest examination as the more specialized aspects are considered in the chapters on the binding of special materials and the repair and care of books. This class of binding falls into two categories— that of preservation and that of extending the useful current working life. Inevitably the two categories are not always clearly distinguishable, but the binding demanded for the two is quite distinct, and it is both inappropriate and extravagant to bind all books as though they were to be used in a century's time. The first category calls for a binding with a long life, the second category calls for a binding that will withstand immediate wear. The popular conception of a binding for posterity was until quite recently a half morocco or half niger binding, but there is a strongly marked reaction against leather for such work in favour of specially treated heavy cloths such as double-warp buckram. Profiting from the experience of our colleagues in the U.S.A., it seems reasonable to specify for such a work a cloth woven with not less than 110 threads per square inch. For the rest of the materials used it is reasonable to specify top-grade material, ensuring that the weight and quality is appropriate. The cost of binding is largely the cost of labour, and it is false economy to save on using strawboard instead of millboard and cotton thread instead of linen thread. It is certainly unwise to use a substitute for gold-leaf, which it is known from experience retains a glow and a clarity over the centuries.

The A.L.A. minimum specification for Class A library binding is particularly useful in the matter of closely specifying standards for bookbinding materials. The techniques used in the application of these materials vary considerably, but it would seem to be agreed that a carefully collated and repaired book, hand sewn on to good quality linen tapes is satisfactory; the heavier volumes should then have the boards either laced on or split boards with the tapes fastened well in should be used.

The binding of books for contemporary use in the reference library should be the same as that adopted for the best type of binding used for non-fiction in the home reading libraries.

This division between the two classes of reference library binding becomes more noticeable in the binding of newspapers and periodicals. It has already been suggested that the selection of newspapers and periodicals for binding should be carried out with considerable care as such material is expensive to bind and difficult to store. If it is also recognized that, in the case of newspapers, some are bound for immediate public use and others are bound for use in half a century's time, it may be that certain newspapers should be bound in duplicate to meet these two quite distinct demands—the popular and the scholarly. To meet current needs a cheap, unsewn, quarter cloth, cut flush binding would usually be adequate. For permanent preservation the file should be well bound with first quality materials by hand craftsmen and provided with a specially made slip case with a drop-down titling flap and strongly reinforced ends at head and tail. Such a slip case would ensure that the volume of newspapers could breathe a little, but would restrict to a minimum the excessive circulation of contaminated air and dust and would also protect the paper against sunshine. The strengthening at the ends of the case would prevent any considerable weight falling on the volume itself when more than one volume is filed to a horizontal shelf. Vertical shelving is most damaging for newspapers as the drag on the top of the book is such that no usable binding can resist it.

Periodicals can also be usefully categorized into those which are required for the current issue only; those which justify filing for up to, say, two years; those which justify filing and binding for up to, say, twenty years of occasional use; and those which represent a useful, permanent addition to the stock of the library. It is an unnecessary extravagance to bind all periodicals as though they were going to be fairly well used for all time. The majority of periodicals bound could, it is suggested, be most usefully and economically bound by unsewn binding in quarter cloth carrying a simple foil blocked label with paper-lined strawboards and cut flush.

For those few periodicals which are to be permanently bound it is necessary to lay down a detailed specification not only of materials and workmanship but also with regard to the lettering and inclusion of advertising material. The instruction might well be on the following lines: Bind according to the agreed specification in full d/w buckram, shade x (specimen herewith), and use lettering in accordance with standardized lettering scheme as laid down by the A.L.A.-L.B.I. Joint Committee. Remove all covers and advertising material except from first and last issues. Bind title-page and index at front of volume, and include supplements and maps at end of volume unless otherwise indicated. Trim initial volume as little as possible, but sufficient to enable standard size to be maintained.

In a chapter largely devoted to a plea for the more careful consideration of material for binding it is appropriate to end with the appeal for more binding of reference material. The older libraries often tend to carry a large book stock, and this book stock is made up not only of the valuable and the significant but the unused and unusable. The Victorian book on cats stands side by side with Beilstein, the tedious reminiscences of the garrulous gardener of the thirties squeeze on the shelf with Humphrey Repton. Most of these books in such libraries have in common their neglect which has produced a rusting of the leather and a falling away of the cloth spine. Many newspaper files of the last century are being hastened into oblivion by a refusal to rebind those volumes which were bound in unsuitable materials and stored on unsuitable shelves.

What is wanted, and what is slowly happening in most libraries, is an increase in the expenditure on new books; a reduction in the number of books bound for home reading; a reappraisal of all newspaper and periodical binding, and a reallocation of binding expenditure so that in general it serves its truer purpose of preserving for posterity rather than attempting to prolong the life of the ephemeral.

CHAPTER THIRTEEN

Unsewn binding

UNSEWN BINDING has been the subject of considerable research since the end of the last war, and occasional references to this technique have appeared in trade and technical journals throughout the world. Inevitably the references give a scanty and quite incomplete picture but taken together with the increased range of machinery designed to produce binding of this type, the announcements by the various manufacturers of adhesives and the increased output of unsewn books, there would seem to be sufficient justification for a careful reassessment of unsewn binding so that librarians may be kept informed of a significant development in book production and bookbinding.

It should be emphasized from the start that those connected with the production, binding, storage and exploitation of books tend to be conservative in their approach, and the suggestion that a technique which has proved itself over many hundreds of years should be changed usually meets with their unequivocal opposition. This, however, is more than offset by the enthusiasm of the convert who believes that the time is not far distant when the folds of his daily newspaper will be trimmed off so that they can be fastened together as single sheets. There is, nevertheless, a substantial group of publishers, bookbinders and librarians who are anxious to know whether unsewn binding is of real value, and some consideration of materials, machinery and techniques used should clearly be the first step in making a reasonable appreciation of the possibilities of unsewn binding.

An article in an American trade journal on "adhesive" binding technique concludes with these words: "If it were not for the gluemaker's ability to concoct flexible, quick-setting adhesives, most of the adhesive binding inventions would be still remaining as just so many entries in the *Patent Gazette*." The development of synthetic adhesives of good ageing properties and increased strength which took place during the last war inevitably led to the consideration of using such adhesives in bookbinding as they have a marked superiority over the ordinary animal glue which is relatively inflexible, tends to lose its efficiency with age, and certainly varies in efficiency according to atmospheric conditions.

For the unsewn binding of books *polyvinyl acetate* emulsions would appear to have made most headway in Great Britain as they have the considerable advantages of being stable, easy of application and not susceptible to mould, bacterial and insect attack. This group of adhesives is manufactured in a very wide range, and care is necessary to ensure that the most appropriate emulsion is used, which would appear to be one which is a mixture of polyvinyl acetate emulsion and polyvinyl alcohol solution with an admixture of plasticizer. These adhesives have the disadvantage of being rather slow to harden, and this has proved to be something of a handicap in their use for high-speed machine production. They also appear to be rather unstable if subjected to low temperatures before use. Their relatively slow drying qualities have proved to be an advantage in hand binding, or for use with simple machines, and this combined with their remarkably consistent performance with varying papers accounts for their present favour.

A good deal of unsewn binding has been carried out with vulcanizable rubber adhesives, and experience with a solution of hycar in a volatile solvent would seem to indicate that this adhesive can provide a remarkably effective bond for this purpose as it combines flexibility with strength and is quick drying. Its ageing qualities for this particular purpose have not been clearly established, but books bound with this material five years ago have not lost their strength nor have the few specimens subjected to artificial ageing tests. Such adhesives have, however, the very real disadvantage of being rather more difficult of application than the first group mentioned, and care has to be taken to avoid fire risks and the danger to the operative of fumes.

In the United States considerable interest has been shown in the use of *hot-melt* adhesives for this type of binding. The essential characteristic of these adhesives is that they are easy of application in their hot-molten state, become viscous at high room temperatures and set almost instantly on cooling. Certain types of hot-melt would seem to be remarkably suitable for unsewn binding as they have a high degree of flexibility, considerable strength and penetration if subjected to hot-rolling after application, and are easy of application. The criticism made of hot-melt is that the range between brittleness and softness is rather too small, but research has been going on for some years and this technique is now used not only for the millions of paper-backed books and magazines such as *Reader's Digest*, but also for a large number of conventionally bound books, and it is claimed that by using a primer it is possible to bind art paper satisfactorily. It seems likely that this adhesive is the answer to the problem of a satisfactory adhesive for high-speed machine production. There is now a machine marketed in the United States which claims to bind 300 books a minute using hot-melt, and one of the largest chemical undertakings in that country is improving and marketing this adhesive.

Animal glues, including the flexible animal glues, are not suitable as they lack the stability, ageing qualities and flexibility which are essential.

MACHINES

Bookbinding machinery would seem to be rather a fashionable business, depending on skilful advertising and so-called sales points rather than a progressive advance as the result of planned and detailed research. This characteristic has the occasional advantage that by proceeding empirically new machines based on old techniques, but using new adhesives, sometimes produce remarkable results.

Essentially the machines fall into three groups: (i) cuts off and roughens the spine and then applies an adhesive with a penetration of about ⅛ inch into the spine; (ii) cuts ⅛-inch slots into the untrimmed signatures, and the adhesive subsequently acts as cords in these slots; (iii) cuts off and fans the spine backwards and forwards so that a strip of adhesive is applied to the back and front of each page.

The majority of these machines are designed for the commercial binder, but an outline of some of the machines on the market today may be of interest to librarians.

The best-known machines are the Perfect Binding Machines manufactured by the T. W. and C. B. Sheridan Co. in the U.S.A. —incidentally, the term *perfect binding* is the monopoly of this company in the U.S.A. These machines are suitable for large plants as their output is estimated to be 300 books per minute, using hot-melt glue two up. The slower and more conventional models run at speeds between 3,000 and 4,000 books per hour, but all follow the same principle of holding the gathered signatures between spring-loaded clamps which then carry the book past the rotary trimmer, the roughening saws and the sheet separators so that the glue may penetrate easily. For certain classes of work it is possible to groove the spine to provide a reinforcing thread of adhesive. After the adhesive has been scraped in, mull, then lining and finally cover are fastened on, or in the case of conventional book production rounding is introduced. This machine is usually operated in conjunction with gathering and covering units.

The British Book Machinery Co. manufactures a number of machines using both animal glues and p.v. acetate emulsion. Production varies from 2,000 to 4,000 books an hour, and like the Sheridan these machines are based on straight-line production which carries the book to a rotary knife for trimming, after which the leaves are deflected for the first application of adhesive, the leaves return to normal for a second coat of adhesive and they are deflected again in the opposite direction for a third coat, after which mull is then applied from a continuous roll and the whole of the spine is pressed and dried. A cutter finally separates the mull linking the books together.

Machines which cut notches into the spine of the signatures are making some headway in the field of unsewn binding. There appear to be two types: the first cut a series of notches about $\frac{1}{8}$ inch deep to produce channels in the spine, and in the second method the notches are arranged in such a way that the gathered book has a series of staggered notches across the spine. The Dexter Cohn Notch Binder will carry out both these processes at speeds of 100–150 signatures per minute two up, and the general trade opinion in the U.S.A. seems to be that the process is versatile for both large and small editions.

There is an interesting compromise between the perfect and

141

the notch binding systems in the pattern roughing machines or the rilled knife machines. These either file or trim off the spine in such a way that the surface of the spine is increased, and in this way has a stronger adhesive surface. The German Masso is an example of this type of machine, and this method is typical of the direction which German binding machinery manufacturers are taking to produce lower cost, simply operated, unsewn binding machinery. It is noteworthy that the principal source of conventional sewing and binding machines is in the eastern zone of Germany, and this appears to have given a marked impetus to research into unsewn techniques. Generally speaking, the German machines are not particularly fast—the most recent machine produced by Hans Ehlermann has an output of 600–850 books an hour—but there are a number of machines by the same manufacturer with much slower output. All of them are based on the principle of trimming off the spine and fanning the leaves so that a film of polyvinyl acetate emulsion is applied to both sides of every leaf. The Rota binder is fully automatic and requires two operatives, and the output is 600–850 books an hour. There are a series of semi-automatic machines of which the Quick is of particular interest as its cost, operation and output of 60–120 books an hour puts it in a class which will interest librarians with binderies. The smallest and simplest machine, the Planatol, is essentially a jig for standardizing and speeding up unsewn binding by hand. It is a small, relatively inexpensive machine, and with an output of 60 books an hour is a useful machine for the small binder. This particular machine is installed in the bindery of Lambeth Public Libraries, where it appears to be quite successful.

TECHNIQUE

The machines producing this type of binding have been given some fairly detailed consideration, but a clearer understanding of the various machines can best be gained by an examination of the methods of binding by hand or by simple machine.

The best known and simplest procedure is to trim off the spine, leaving it flush. The possibility of notching with or without trimming off the spine was the subject of experiments some years ago, and the results all seemed to point to the bond strength being in direct proportion to the length of the bond. It would seem to follow that there are advantages in increasing the surface area to be fastened by the adhesive as far as is consistent with an efficient book, and it would also seem to follow that so long as other factors do not affect the bond then use of unsewn binding for large folios is a reasonable proposition.

The problem of increasing the surface area has been tackled in a number of ways. There is the rilled knife, the notching, the roughening and the fanning of the leaves, and these latter two have been widely used in hand binding. The procedure in the small library bindery is usually to trim off the spines of two books at a time, and they are tightly clamped about two inches from the spines, which are then roughened by a grinding wheel or rasp and a thinned coat of adhesive is brushed on. The leaves are fanned out by pressing them to the right or left so that one side of each leaf receives a fine margin of thinned adhesive, the leaves are fanned in the opposite direction and the first thinned coat of adhesive is completed. The purpose of this first coat is to give increased protection and serve as a key for the second and third coats, which consist of the adhesive at normal strength applied in just the same way as the thinned layer. Immediately after the second coat the mull or flexible canvas is pressed on leaving an overlap of about one inch at front and back. The obvious tendency to strengthen this material must be resisted as the adhesive has to penetrate quickly and completely. Stronger material inevitably slows down this process and produces an ineffective hinge.

The rounding and backing of the book can take place any time within the course of the next twenty-four hours, and it would seem that the traditional manually operated backing press and hammer are as quick and efficient as the mechanical backing press for the process.

From this point the book proceeds as though conventionally bound or cased.

PAPER

Unsewn binding is similar to sewn binding in that it binds some paper more efficiently than others and generally speaking, it would seem to have the same weaknesses. Until quite recently it was thought that unsewn binding was ineffective with books which contained an insert of paper for illustrations usually of a fairly high calendered nature, but it is noticeable that the commercial binder who binds Penguin-Pelican books appears to have overcome this difficulty.

Experiments and checks made on the various papers point quite definitely to the conclusion that a good quality antique wove is the most suitable paper for unsewn binding, followed by cartridge and litho papers. Imitation art is superior to genuine art paper, but quite the most unsuitable paper is machine coated. The key to suitability would seem to be the surface absorption of the paper.

CONCLUSION

The very considerable headway made during the past six or seven years by unsewn binding has largely been in the binding of paper-backed editions, but an increasing number of publishers are turning to it for an occasional hard-backed edition, and if this increases, and it seems reasonable that it should, librarians and bookbinders will need to give a great deal more thought to this problem of how to bind together a loose set of leaves.

Unsewn binding is not likely to prove an answer to all our binding problems as it merely substitutes a different set of problems for the existing ones, but it has the considerable advantage of being cheaper at certain levels of production.

Certainly the commercial binders will need to face the problem boldly, and there is little doubt that they will do so. At present they display an understandable reluctance to advance a technique which will ultimately necessitate a large measure of retooling in their factories, but this will presumably be met by the enterprise of small firms who are not faced with such problems of capital expenditure.

For the library bindery unsewn binding has many advantages. In the first place, it enables the authority to establish a library bindery as an economic unit when it only requires to rebind, say, 20,000 volumes a year, whereas the traditional library bindery needs an output of 30,000 volumes a year to operate economically. This is achieved by reducing the size of the team required to staff the bindery. The small library bindery using, for example, a

Planatol machine should be able to produce 20,000 volumes per annum. It may very well be that as the bindery expands and the output increases to more than 40,000 volumes per annum the unsewn technique can be replaced by the sewn, and by the introduction of several machines, but this is a complex problem depending upon many factors and the extent to which publishers use unsewn binding initially. Certainly it is possible to visualize a further stage of development using an unsewn binding machine to produce 75,000 re-bound volumes a year, which would then, in time, replace the sewing machine.

It is necessary that all who are concerned with books should examine critically any developments which are likely to make it possible to circulate books more readily. On the one hand there seems to be little point in a stern refusal even to consider the possibilities of unsewn binding, but there is of course the other over-enthusiastic point of view represented by the writer in the house journal of the Du Pont de Nemours Co. who concludes: "Millions of paper back and hard cover books and magazines like the *Reader's Digest* are being bound faster, more economically and more permanently with these rugged new chemical adhesives. Their future seems limited only by the requirements of those craftsmen who took over from the monks more than 500 years ago."

Mr. Richard Clay is one of the leading British bookbinders of publishers' editions today, and although it would be wrong to assume that he speaks on behalf of all such binders his views on unsewn binding are most forthright: "I nail my flag firmly to the mast of the so-called 'unsewn binding', although I do not accept the present stage as by any means final. The basic idea of taking your preassembled book block into one lump and welding it into a homogeneous mass in one operation is the greatest piece of work simplification that has been achieved for many years, and the principle of treating a book block in this way is likely to form the basis of future developments for some time to come."

CHAPTER FOURTEEN

Recent developments

THE ARCHIVIST of the United States of America in his Third Annual Report 1936–37 wrote: "Perhaps, as has been said, archivists trained in older methods may 'shake a conservative head' over the ultra-modern methods of the National Archives, less conservative heads will recall, however, that all other methods of repair were also once ultra-modern and may well question whether, before they were adopted, any of them were subjected to such thorough tests as the one under suspicion."

This comment was on the practice adopted by the National Archives of the U.S. of reinforcement or repair of fragile or damaged papers by mounting them under heat and pressure between sheets of cellulose acetate film, a technique which will be considered in greater detail later in this chapter.

It is inevitable that librarians and archivists, concerned as they are with the task of preserving written and printed records for posterity, should ensure that new methods and new materials have been fully tested before they are used. In the United States the National Bureau of Standards does a great deal of testing of both techniques and materials, and the Library Binding Institute also concerns itself with the value and wearing qualities of new materials and new methods. Some of the larger industrial under-takings such as Du Pont de Nemours are conducting research into adhesives and advanced bookbinding machinery. In Great Britain the Printing, Packaging and Allied Trades Research Association (PATRA) carries out most of the testing of both new materials and new methods, and in addition to their substantial contribution in this field they have also made considerable advances in the develop-ment of existing materials and methods. Its findings are made available to the Government through the Department of Scientific and Industrial Research and to the trade through the employers' associations and, occasionally, directly to the producer. The range

of research carried out by these various organizations is considerable, and the greater part of it is outside the scope of this book,
but librarians are quite reasonably concerned with such new techniques as unsewn binding, which is dealt with in a separate
chapter, and variations in the conventional bookbinding techniques. They are also concerned with new materials, particularly
with substitute bookbinding materials and protective materials
such as transparent films. It is in this latter category that some of
the most significant developments have taken place in the past ten
years, and brief consideration will first be given to the development and qualities of these films followed by a more detailed
consideration of their application to bookbinding, book repair
and the preservation of documents.

TRANSPARENT FILMS

Cellulose film has been manufactured commercially for nearly
half a century and is made from the same raw material as paper,
for the cellulose fibres which are matted to form a sheet of paper
also provide the basis of this type of film. The process of converting the fibres into transparent film is lengthy and complicated,
involving the steeping, shredding and conversion into a solution
known as viscone, which is subsequently extruded to convert it
to film.

Today this film is made in a limited range of thicknesses
between 0·00085 and 0·0016 inch, but there is a wide variety of
treatments, most of which are designed to produce a moisture-
proof film. This treatment widens the possible applications as
untreated the film absorbs moisture and becomes highly flexible.
It is in any case a fairly flexible film of great strength when dry or
when moisture-proofed. Its other advantages are that it can
be easily sealed with conventional adhesives when untreated
and it is fairly resistant to grease. One or two of the newer
cellulose films—such as SMAT grades—can be heat-sealed,
and the majority of cellulose films which cannot be sealed with
conventional adhesives can be successfully sealed with polymer
adhesives.

The film is cheap, readily available in most grades and manufactured in reels or sheets up to about 48 inches, under a wide

147

variety of trade names, including Cellophane, Rayofilm, Viscascelle, and when used as a self-adhesive tape, Sellotape.

Cellulose acetate is also made from cellular fibres, but in this case the raw material comes from cotton linters, which are produced from the waste fibres left on the cotton seed after it has passed through the ginning machine used to grade and clean raw cotton.

The fibres are broken down and dissolved in acetic acid, and the solution is washed before it is extruded in sheet form after which it is pressed and rolled.

It is manufactured in a wide variety of thicknesses, ranging from 0·001 to 0·005 inch, and the finished product is a clear, hard, glossy film. It has little tear strength and is almost as hygroscopic as cellulose, but it does not stretch so much when moist. It is not readily inflammable, and if carefully made it has excellent ageing qualities and is so suitable that it can be used for the preservation of valuable documents.

The sealing of this inexpensive film is rather difficult as the application of p.v.a. adhesive tends to produce rippling and distortion which are rather difficult to overcome without the proper machinery and techniques. Heat and pressure sealing of the untreated film is possible with certain specially prepared grades, but it calls for an exact application of heat at a temperature between 150°C. and 175°C. and a pressure range varying between 300 and 2,000 pounds per square inch. The conventional method of laminating paper with cellulose acetate is by using the film treated with specially prepared wax adhesive, and it can then be heat-sealed efficiently over quite a wide range of temperatures.

The film is fairly cheap, but demand is high and delivery is occasionally rather slow as a consequence. It is manufactured in rolls of up to 4 feet and is sold under a variety of trade names such as Acetophane, Clarifoil, Rhodoid, and Utilex. The prepared film with the wax adhesive is manufactured under the name Morane.

Cellulose nitrate is also made from cellular waste material, but the basis can be wood or cotton or waste cellulose film.

It is used as a film base for photographic purposes, but its inflammability and the fact that it results in deterioration of paper and cannot be satisfactorily manufactured in thicknesses of o·oo1 inch or thereabouts precludes its use for reinforcing documents and the like. It provides a strong, cheap, transparent film for protecting maps from damage when being traced and as a shield for guides, etc., but it tends to discolour when exposed to strong sunlight for prolonged periods.

This film is most frequently used today after it has been specially treated with wax as a cheap and effective food wrapping, but it does not appear to be particularly suitable in its present form for many of the uses to which films can be put in the library. It is manufactured under the general names of Celluloid and Xylonite.

Polyvinylchloride. Although this polymer was discovered a century ago it has only been used commercially for twenty years, but in that time it has established itself as one of the most useful types of film, and its applications in the field of clothing, industrial fittings and insulation are widely appreciated. In its unplasticized state it is inflexible and is only used when a material with a high melting-point and marked resistance to chemical action is required. When the polymer is plasticized the qualities vary with the plasticizer used, but the finished product is usually flexible, non-inflammable, hard-wearing and resistant to water and corrosion.

The film made from this material is produced by calendering the plasticized mixture, and it can be heat-sealed either by high frequency or by a press equipped with a special barrier to prevent the film adhering to the heat jaws. A more usual method is by sewing the sheets together, and this is possible because of the remarkable tear strength of properly plasticized grades.

It has an attractive matt surface, but in the more hard-wearing qualities it is usually slightly opaque. The grades used in connection with the protection of books and printed materials are readily available in a wide range of both thicknesses and widths. It is usually marketed just as P.V.C. film, but there are a number of branded films under such names as Corilite, Duvina, and Corvic.

Polythene is also referred to occasionally as polyethylene and has only been manufactured for general sale since the last war. Basically it is the simplest of synthetic polymers, but the manufacture of it calls for elaborate high-pressure equipment. The soft granules of the polymer are made into film either by extrusion or calendering, but it is usual for the clearer films to be made by extrusion into water as a continuous tube. This tubing is then either trimmed into sheet form up to 6 feet wide or sold in "layflat" tubing from 1 to 40 inches wide. The thicknesses range from 0·0015 to 0·010 inch.

Polythene film has a pleasantly matt surface and is not quite as clear as, for example, cellulose acetate. It is, however, chemically inert and is resistant to acids, soaps and detergents, animal and vegetable oils, and is almost completely waterproof. Unfortunately it is not scratch-resistant.

Heat-sealing can be carried out by most of the conventional pressure machines, and it can also be sealed by applying a very high temperature (570°F.) with a light pressure for a short time. Unfortunately this strong and versatile film cannot be readily and satisfactorily laminated with paper, but the development of spraying paper with alkathene which has recently been announced may subsequently be of interest and value to librarians.

The I.C.I. patent for the manufacture of polythene has just expired and four other undertakings have announced their intention of manufacturing this polymer although not necessarily by the I.C.I. process. At present the finished film is marketed under such names as Diothene and Telcothene.

The plastic industry is vigorous and ingenious, and from its laboratories flow a steady stream of new polymers and new applications for older materials. In a summary of this kind it would be inappropriate to attempt to give an appreciation of most of the materials which are at present, or may in the near future be, used for the production of protective films. The only really outstanding development of a new type of film which may prove to be of considerable interest to librarians but has not yet been marketed is that of polyethylene and terephthalate. This material was discovered in 1941, and the rights to develop the invention in this country have passed to I.C.I., who are marketing it under the name of terylene. The production and experimental research is at present largely concerned with Terylene fibre, but experiments have shown that the film from this polymer possesses remarkable qualities, being light in weight, tough, tear- and scratch-resistant, and non-absorbent. The pilot plant of the I.C.I. has produced film 0·00025 inch thick, and it seems that these finer gauges are superior in strength to any comparable film. It is not at present available for commercial use.

Applications. These films can be applied either as a loose protective cover or so that they form a lamination with the paper or other material covered. They can be and are used for such purposes as protecting book jackets, protecting manuscripts and rare documents, reinforcing sheet music, maps, newspapers and other material.

Book jackets. There is an obvious irony in this accretion of protective material around the actual text of a book. Title-page is followed by half-title-page, which in turn is followed by paper cover, then boards, then cloth or leather, then dust jacket and finally protection for the dust jacket. In spite of this the intention is sound enough as the aim must be to maintain the book in as clean and attractive a state as possible during the course of its useful life.

As a reaction against the soiled book stocks and the standardized binding of the war years, there was a move by some public libraries towards the preservation of the book jacket, and during the past ten years this has resulted in three types of protection for the book jacket: (i) the incorporation of the book jacket as part of the book case itself and the protection of this jacket with a strong transparent protective film; (ii) the fitting or covering of the jacket with a transparent protective film and subsequently fastening down inside the boards the protective jacket or fitting the boards into sleeves behind the book jacket; (iii) the lamination of the book jacket with a transparent film and reinforcing this jacket with a backing of additional paper to serve both as a reinforcement and a flap to take the surplus film. The jacket is subsequently fastened down inside the boards.

Of these three methods the first is both the strongest and the most expensive. It has the obvious disadvantage that it can only be used either for a limited range of new titles or, if it is used for rebinding, it necessitates keeping and filing the original book jacket or obtaining a further copy from the publisher. In spite of these disadvantages there is little doubt that when some small technical and production difficulties are overcome this technique will be used extensively to produce library editions that are both attractive and durable.

A number of materials have been used with varying degrees of success. Polythene, which would appear to be the most suitable, was first used to form a lamination with the book jacket, and a reinforcing piece of paper which projected beyond the book added to give a turn-in when the case was made. In the making of this case the laminated book jacket was used as cloth is normally used. Unfortunately although strong and attractive, the film occasionally tended to yellow and bubble, and production has for the moment ceased.

Cellulose acetate has also been used, particularly with larger covers on cut flush bindings, the method used being to fasten the film by adhesive, heat and pressure to either the book jacket or the paper cover and then to mount this lamination on board. This material has also been used to protect the jacket mounted on library cloth to form a case in the conventional way, but the sharp folding at head and tail of spine tends to crack the film. Paper-backed books are also being processed and marketed in this way with rather more success.

Polyvinyl chloride can be effectively heat-sealed, and when treated in this way it can provide a strong and fairly attractive matt cover for the book jacket, and this covered book jacket can then be used instead of a piece of cloth to form a case covering. The edge seal used tends to give a small but rather unsightly projection all round the book, but this will almost certainly be overcome in the near future. Meanwhile this material would seem to be the one most likely to be used for library editions in what our American colleagues call "illustrated covers".

The second method is widely used today, and many of the library booksellers supply their books protected in this way if they are asked to do so. One or two independent suppliers specialize in the marketing of these plastic sleeves or book vests as they are sometimes called. The simplest type consists of a layflat tube, usually of polyvinyl chloride or polythene, and the jacket is placed flat inside the tube which is then trimmed off at each end. The jacket, sandwiched in the film which varies in thickness between 0·001 and 0·002 inch, is then fitted back over the book, either by fastening it down inside the boards with adhesive tape or a special adhesive, or by sliding the boards of the book into the opened ends of the tube behind the book jacket. The obvious disadvantage of such protection is that it is not hospitable to the considerable variations in book sizes and requires a large number of tubes of varying widths if the protected book is to have a finished neat appearance. The difficulty has been overcome to some extent by sewing at head and tail a piece of polythene about 9 inches wide to strips of cover paper 4½ inches wide, and these flaps are then folded and fastened together over the book jacket so that they provide a neatly fitting sleeve. The usual practice is to slide the boards into the open ends of the tube, but it would seem that the more neatly fitting the tube the more difficulty there is in inserting the boards into the end of the sleeve. Also falling into this category is the specially tailored book vest such as the one manufactured under the trade name of Kleersheel. In this type instead of fitting the book jacket inside a tube of film the boards of the book complete with book jacket are slid into the two pockets of the book vest, and so give a strong and fairly complete protection so long as the size of the book is fairly close to the various sizes of the book vest. There are at present three sizes and they are reasonably expandable.

The considerable advantage of these methods is that they can be introduced without special machinery or special techniques. The cost varies from 1½d. for a piece of layflat polythene tubing suitable for a demy octavo to 8½d. for a tailored book vest, and in both cases the cost of fitting would need to be added. A more general price would seem to be 6d. per volume, including fitting by the library bookseller.

The third method is the most economical and in some ways the most satisfactory in that it can be applied to book jackets of all shapes and sizes. It consists of a film of cellulose acetate 0·001 or 0·0015 inch in thickness fastened to the book jacket and reinforced by backing paper. The film is fastened either by liquid adhesive applied to the film and then brought into contact with the jacket or by means of a specially prepared film carrying a wax-type adhesive which is subsequently used to form an effective lamination with heat and pressure. The use of a liquid adhesive demands special skills and special machinery, but it is extremely cheap, costing less than 2*d.* a volume. The film carrying the wax-type adhesive can be purchased already prepared and then fixed to the jacket by means of a heated press. The average cost of such a lamination is 3*d.* After lamination the jacket and its reinforcing paper is fastened to the book by means of adhesive tape. The protected book is likely to give at least thirty issues before there is any deterioration.

It will be seen that all these methods are designed not only to produce a cleaner, fresher book stock but also to lengthen the useful life of the publisher's case and its covering book jacket.

PRESERVATION OF DOCUMENTS

This chapter was introduced with a quotation from the report of the Archivist of the United States for 1936–37 on the lamination of fragile and damaged papers with sheets of cellulose acetate film. The report continues: "The method adopted by the National Archives was developed, thoroughly tested and approved by the National Bureau of Standards. . . . Tests show that a document treated by this method may be cleaned by soap and water, is practically impervious to gases, and will be relatively unaffected by the normal processes of deterioration."

The National Archives of the United States has been laminating papers with cellulose acetate since 1936 and is still continuing to do so. Mr. Wayne C. Grover, the Archivist, writes: "However, an investigation of cellulose acetate and its overall permanency is again being conducted by the National Bureau of Standards for the National Archives so that we may be even more sure of its permanency. This investigation will also include products or materials which do not require a plasticizer for maintaining their flexibility, yet which can be applied by lamination."

Although the National Archives have been using this process for nearly twenty years various other agencies were using similar techniques, both in this country and America before 1936. The most widely used is the method already described in Chapter XI on the repair and care of books, whereby a net of fine silk gauze is fastened to the surface of the documents with a carefully made paste. Other similar methods include the use of Japanese tissue or a similar tough transparent paper. Experiments have been carried out with cellulose film and cellulose nitrate, but it has been found that the former is inferior to cellulose acetate for this purpose as it tends to wrinkle with age, and cellulose nitrate should not be used as prolonged contact will result in a marked deterioration of the paper so covered.

In considering the most suitable material for this important work the permanence is the key factor, but weight, thickness and cost are secondary considerations.

The permanence of all such materials can readily be challenged. The fine silk gauze is fastened with a dextrine which even when treated with paranitrophenol may ultimately be susceptible to attack by fungi and bacteria. Certainly as a covering material it is rather bulky, adding 0·003 inch when carefully applied with reasonable pressure, but it is fairly light in weight. Japanese tissue is usually also fastened with dextrine, but this is only 0·002 inch when carefully applied and is even lighter than silk gauze, but both these methods result in some slight deterioration in legibility and tend to obscure ultra-violet and infra-red light rays when these are used to decipher damaged or faded writing or printing.

Many advantages are claimed for lamination with cellulose acetate film, but there is first the considerable disadvantage of being three times the weight of Japanese tissue and more than twice the weight of silk gauze. This is offset to some extent by the fact that the thickness of film normally used is 0·001 inch, and consequently it occupies much less space. The advantages claimed for it are considerable. It can be applied fairly cheaply and quickly to large quantities of documents by heat and pressure. It produces a perfectly transparent cover which actually increases legibility and improves colour values and at the same time this film covering does not impair the transmission of ultra-violet or infra-red rays. Finally it produces a record which is protected against the risks of water, staining and discoloration through atmospheric impurities or gases.

The National Bureau of Standards of the United States has carried out a comprehensive programme of tests of the use of cellulose acetate film for this purpose, and the conclusion reached was that both film applied by heat and pressure and film applied with an adhesive and heat and pressure had a sufficiently high degree of stability to be suitable for use with permanent records, and that the film used had no adverse effect upon the stability of the paper.

THE PROTECTION OF MAPS, MUSIC AND NEWSPAPERS AND OTHER PRINTED SURFACES

Any unprotected printing surface which is subject to excessive wear can be protected and strengthened by the use of a carefully applied transparent surface. This additional surface can best be provided by a film such as those already mentioned with particular emphasis on cellulose acetate.

A film such as cellulose acetate if correctly fastened to the surface either by means of liquid or wax adhesive will enhance the colour value of the printed surface and add considerably to its strength. Such a process is of value for heavily used street plans and ordnance survey maps.

If sheet music is protected on both sides it gives a lamination of considerable strength so that the music is more serviceable to the reader and can be issued forty or more times. Newspapers can also be laminated in this way, but the cost is likely to be prohibitive for anything other than rare or early issues as a single page of *The Times* would cost approximately 3s. 3d. if covered on two sides.

FELTED FIBRES

This is a material which is being increasingly widely used for the making of book-cloth substitutes, as a basis for imitation leather, and in place of mull in publisher's casing. It consists of synthetic fibres felted together in sheets and then laminated to give strength. One of these bonded fibre fabrics is made from regenerated cellulose, and the finished product is fairly strong and durable.

Impregnated with appropriate fillers, it is in use as a substitute for book cloths and leathers, and appears to serve admirably for the purpose, the cloth being easy to print and the leather easy to work.

Untreated, the material is much cheaper than mull but stronger than paper, and occasionally publishers are using the parallel laid bonded fibre fabric to form an effective joint to link the case with the book.

REINFORCING JOINTS

A little practical experience of the wearing qualities of books will soon show that the spine of the case and the inner joints tend to weaken first. It is only recently that any serious thought has

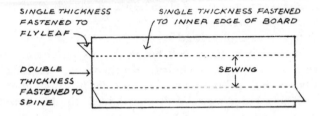

SINGLE THICKNESS FASTENED TO FLYLEAF

SINGLE THICKNESS FASTENED TO INNER EDGE OF BOARD

DOUBLE THICKNESS FASTENED TO SPINE

SEWING

REINFORCING TAPE

been given to the protection of the spine, but over many years occasional efforts have been made to strengthen the inner joints of a publisher's case. The obvious way was to fasten down a strip of cloth or strong paper reinforcing tape so that it overlapped a little on to the fly-leaves and the pasted down endpapers, but as is often the case in a nicely balanced structure the effect of such patching was merely to throw the strain a few pages away towards the centre of a book—to a point, in fact, less able than the original joint to take the strain. There seems no reasonable possibility of any satisfactory method being devised whereby a casing is strengthened by an application of material at the inner joints.

An interesting experiment in reinforcing a publisher's casing was carried out before the last war and modified recently so that it reinforces the whole of the sewn spine and the inner surface of the spine of the case, and then provides new inner joints of double linen fastened down on to the fly-leaves and pasted down end-papers. The tape used consists of a sewn tube of linen with flaps, and the width between the sewing of the tube varies with the thickness of the spine. These tapes are usually sewn up in lengths of fifty yards or so in a wide range of sizes. These sizes vary by $\frac{1}{8}$ of an inch from a width of $\frac{1}{4}$ inch to 2 inches between the sewing.

To fit the tube the book is neatly cut out of the case at the inner joint, and the tube is then glued on to the spine, covering the lining up or the sewing, and the inner flaps are fastened down on the fly-leaves. The outer surface of the tube is glued up and the case pressed on by pressing down the spine and the boards. The book is then subjected to quick pressure in a small nipping press and placed in a standing press to dry.

If the tape is carefully fitted so that the sewing fits well into the inner joint and it is then well fastened, this reinforcement can produce a book that is much stronger than a conventional publisher's case, but if the tape does not fit precisely there will inevitably be a tendency to pull the body of the book with the consequent weakening of the sewing.

Such a technique would seem likely to be of most value for many juvenile books before they pass into circulation, but even so discretion is called for as there are publishers of children's books who produce a fairly strong and workmanlike case which it would be foolish to reinforce unnecessarily.

Adult books can in the majority of cases be left unreinforced, but it is often possible to reinforce such books after they have been issued twenty or thirty times, and the opportunity should then be taken to glue up the spines and clean the edges before having them reinforced. The reinforced book in a clean publisher's case can then be returned to circulation for thirty to forty issues and subsequently discarded or re-bound. Such a procedure could revolutionize the appearance of the shelves of home reading libraries and would in many cases result in substantial economies.

A STATISTICAL ANALYSIS OF LIBRARY BINDERIES
ADMINISTERED BY PUBLIC LIBRARY AUTHORITIES

QUESTIONNAIRES WERE circulated to fourteen library authorities maintaining library binderies, but it was found that only eleven of the replies could be included in this statistical analysis, and even so it must be emphasized that special circumstances apply in each case, and the figures are designed to show general trends and variations in organization, output, costs, staffing and equipment as they were in 1955.

Key to categories

A With an annual output exceeding 35,000 re-bound volumes per annum.
B With an annual output exceeding 20,000 re-bound volumes per annum.
C With an annual output exceeding 10,000 re-bound volumes per annum.
D Craft bindery concerned largely with special binding and repairs.
E Repair shop not specializing in rebinding but carrying out repairs, reinforcing and special work.
F Bindery specializing in strengthening and protecting new books.

Key to machinery

a Sewing machine—Martini, Brehmer, etc.
b Book smasher—Garatt, etc.
c Guillotine—power-operated
d Guillotine—hand-operated
e Board cutter
f Rounder and backer
g Rounding machine—hand
h Backing machine—hand
i Gluing machine
j Nipping press
k Blocking press

159

Notes

1.   The books re-bound include 110 volumes of newspapers, some of which needed extensive repair, costing up to £30 per volume.

2.   Miscellaneous work includes: 13 boxes and 18 binders.

3.   Miscellaneous work includes: 128 cases, 139 maps dissected and mounted, 352 mounts, 155 boxes and 199 miscellaneous items.

4.   Miscellaneous work includes: 23 magazine cases, 54 boxes for sets of plays, 179 dummy books, also mounting maps, displays, etc.

5.   Miscellaneous work includes: 1,500 quarter cloth cases with tapes, 69 blotting-pads, 24 pamphlet boxes, 139 pamphlet boxes repaired, 4,121 plastic jackets and 430 maps dissected, mounted and cased.

6.   Miscellaneous work includes: (i) 16,217 volumes strengthened by sewing in new reinforced endpapers, gluing up spine, replacing mull and pasting down; (ii) cutting up stationery; (iii) making of special volumes for music in parts; (iv) pamphlet cases.

7.   Strengthening and cost of plastic jacket (approximately 7¼d.) per volume is responsible for £700 under cost of materials.

8.   Includes detailed overhead charges made up as follows: (i) Proportion of salary of Chief Librarian (2 per cent); (ii) Proportion of salaries of Stock Editor and Assistants (20 per cent); (iii) Proportion of cost of inter-library transport (50 per cent); and (iv) Proportion of Central Library administrative expenses (£162).

9.   Includes an allowance for superannuation and plant renewals.

10.   Librarian states that this accommodation is quite inadequate.

	A	B (i)	B (ii)	B (iii)	B (iv)	C (i)	C (ii)	C (iii)	D	E	F
Books—re-bound	38,422	20,057	20,044	21,658	20,047	10,500	14,312	14,258	2,781[1]	1,860	4,536
resewn	72	—	—	—	4,979	—	—	—	—	1,902	—
recased	—	—	—	—	15,068	—	—	—	—	—	4,549
repaired	431	—	—	18,974	132	—	4,875	—	23	—	—
numbered	40,000	20,117[2]	—	21,658[3]	4,710	35,000	13	—	—	—	39,146[6]
labelled	70,000	—	100	—	—[4]	35,000	—	—	—	—	—
Miscellaneous items	1,150[2]	—	—	—	—	—	—	—[5]	—	—	—
Estimated value of output	11,000	6,822	—	—	—	—	3,650	2,193	—	—	—
Average cost of binding (s. d.)											
(a) fiction	3 3	4 8½	3 6	4 4½	4 4	4 9	4 0½	3 1	—	—	2 1[7]
(b) non-fiction	5 6	9 5	—	—	—	7 5	—	—	—	5 8	3 8
Cost of library bindery (£)											
(a) Wages	6,023	3,850	4,013	3,815	3,590	2,660	2,021	2,167	2,300	913	1,620
(b) Materials	1,706	1,462	805	924	703	200	430	701	634	220	1,210[7]
(c) Lighting, etc.	125	132	36	—	100	25	—	228	75	—	70
(d) Rent, rates, etc.	100	175	70	—	—	25	—	1	71	49	25
(e) Other charges	200	50	818[8]	—	12	700[9]	340	104	—	—	475
TOTAL	8,154	5,559	5,742	4,739	4,405	3,610	2,791	3,200	3,080	1,182	3,405
Number of staff											
(a) Males	7	5	5	3	5	3	3	3	3	1	2
(b) Apprentices	2	—	—	1	1	—	—	—	1	1	—
(c) Females	10	3	3	8	4	4	2	2	3	2	5
(d) Learners	(brace)	—	—	4	—	—	—	—	1	—	7
TOTAL	19	8	8	16	10	7	5	5	8	4	7
Floor space in square feet	4,500	850	900[10]	1,500	1,408	600	880	350	2,100	400	460
Machinery	aceijk	acefk	abcefik	ach	d	acef	c	cehk	cghjk	dej	ck

MINIMUM SPECIFICATION FOR CLASS "A" LIBRARY BINDING

ISSUED BY THE JOINT COMMITTEE OF THE AMERICAN LIBRARY ASSOCIATION AND THE LIBRARY BINDING INSTITUTE

PART I. CLASSIFICATION OF VOLUMES

For the purpose of these specifications, the different types of volume are defined as follows:

Ordinary book-volume. Any ordinary-sized graphic material consisting of an appreciable number of leaves or folded sheets produced originally as a unit, and submitted for binding or rebinding as such a unit according to accepted standardized methods, and not requiring special handling. (An ordinary book-volume ranges in height from about 6 inches to 12 inches, with width in proportion, and thickness not exceeding 2 inches.)

Ordinary magazine-volume. A series of multi-leaved, like-constituted, serially-numbered graphic units submitted for binding or rebinding into a scheduled multi-unit volume and not requiring special handling. (An ordinary magazine-volume ranges in height from about 8 inches to 16 inches, with width in proportion and thickness not exceeding 2½ inches.)

Ordinary newspaper-volume. A series of newspaper-issues (or other serial publication printed on newsprint) arranged for binding into a composite unit bulking not more than 2 inches, and not requiring special handling.

Special volume. Any undersized, over-sized and odd-sized volume or any volume that requires special handling, in any of the three classifications. The binder shall arrange specifically with the library as to the nature of the special work to be done or shall exercise his best technical judgment as to the requirements of a particular special volume. (For instance, a special book-volume, because of size or technical nature, may equal or even exceed a magazine-volume in difficulty of handling and therefore in the value of the work. Similarly a special magazine-volume may require more work, at a higher value, than a newspaper volume. These specifications do not attempt to cover all kinds of special work; but the approved methods of handling the most frequent kinds are specified.)

PART II. REBINDING BOOKS

1. *Collating and Mending*

(*a*) All books shall be carefully collated before being taken apart to detect any missing or damaged leaves or any peculiarities of paper or construction that might make rebinding inadvisable.

(*b*) All tears through print shall be mended with Japanese tissue or onionskin bond, and all tears in margins with bond paper of suitable weight.

2. *Preparation for Sewing*

(*a*) All double leaves, maps or inserts shall be set out with strips of bond paper, or equal.

(*b*) Books unsuited for oversewing shall be prepared and reinforced for sewing through their folded sections.

3. *Removing Backs*

For books that are to be oversewed, folds on the back shall be sanded off with a sand wheel, or removed by taking a very narrow trim, not more than $\frac{1}{16}$ inch, so as to leave all back margin possible.

4. *Dividing into Sections*

(*a*) Books that are to be oversewed shall be divided into uniform sections, each section not to exceed 0·050 inch in thickness, except flexible pulpy paper which may be in thicker sections not to exceed 0·060 inch each.

(*b*) All sections of books in which paper is moderately stiff shall be scored before sewing. (Extra stiff papers unless hinged shall not be oversewed; usually these may be sewed through their folded sections after necessary reinforcement of folds.)

5. *Endpapers*

(*a*) All endpapers shall consist of three functional parts; a pasted-down or outward end-leaf which becomes the cover lining; at least two free fly-leaves; and reinforcing fabric.

(*b*) The following three types of endpapers shall be permissible:

Type X. Three-leaf; single reinforcement; invisible joint; with the inward fly-leaf not pasted to the middle leaf.

Type Y. Three-leaf; single reinforcement; visible joint; with the inward fly-leaf not pasted to the middle leaf.

Type Z. Four-leaf; double reinforcement; visible joint; with the two middle leaves pasted together forming a single leaf.

(*c*) The construction of endpapers shall be such that the sewing will go through the reinforcing fabric the same as through the sections of the book.

6. *Sewing*

(*a*) Most books having proper inner margins and suitable paper shall be sewed with thread by oversewing method, either by machine or by hand. If sewed by machine, all sections shall be pasted. As many needles shall be used as possible, providing that this does not bring the sewing closer to the head and tail of the book than $\frac{1}{4}$ inch after trimming.

(*b*) Exceptional books such as little folks' picture books, music, certain art books and some reference books, shall be sewed through their folded sections. When such sewing is used, weak folds of sections shall be reinforced with strips of bond paper, and the sewing shall be done on three or more tapes or cords with linen thread, usually one-on.

7. *Trimming*

All books shall be trimmed as slightly as possible (or left untrimmed if so instructed).

8. *Edges*

Edges shall be sprinkled, stained or left plain as instructed.

9. *Gluing, Rounding, Backing and Lining*

Backs of books shall be glued with approved flexible glue, well rounded and backed, and lined with approved Canton flannel extending to within $\frac{1}{4}$ inch of head and tail of books, and well on to each endpaper (approximately $1\frac{1}{2}$ inches).

10. *Covers*

(*a*) Covers shall be made of heavy-weight starch-filled or pyroxylin-filled buckram or drill base pyroxylin-coated material of a quality at least equal to the standards set forth in Part V of these specifications.

(*b*) Covers shall be made over hard-rolled binders board, with uniform squares, in a neat and workmanlike manner. The thickness of the board shall be suited to the size and weight of the book.

(*c*) The cover material shall be turned in enough to insure proper adhesion (normally $\frac{5}{8}$ inch is necessary).

11. *Inlays*

All covers shall have an inlay of flexible paper securely attached to the inside of the backbone of the cover. The paper shall be cut the same length as the cover boards, and the approximate width of the back of the book after it has been rounded and backed. The paper shall be of a thickness appropriate to the thickness of the cover boards but not less than 0·01 (one hundredth) of an inch.

12. Casing In

Books shall be cased in with glycol paste, or equal, and pressed between metal-edged boards until thoroughly dry.

13. Lettering

(a) Lettering shall be done after proper sizing in clear type of a size appropriate to the book, in style and position as instructed, using X.X. 23-carat gold deeply impressed to insure long adhesion to the cover.

(b) At the option of the library, approved colored foils or inks may be used; but no gold-colored substitute of any kind may be used without the express approval of the library.

14. Protective Lacquering of Backs

All books shall be sprayed or treated with a protective material evenly and lightly applied over their lettered backs.

15. Inspection

All books shall be carefully opened out and critically inspected for defects in binding or errors in lettering.

PART III. BINDING MAGAZINES

1. Collating and Mending

(a) All issues shall be carefully examined to detect any damage or any peculiarities of paper or construction in order to determine the most suitable method of binding or the necessity for special handling.

(b) All issues shall be carefully checked and collated for proper sequence, pagination, title-page, index, inserts and supplements. Incompleteness or defects shall be reported.

(c) Inclusion or omission of covers, advertising and similar material shall be handled in accordance with instructions.

(d) Foreign language and technical magazines shall be given such special checking and collation as may be necessitated by the nature of the contents.

(e) All tears through print shall be mended with Japanese tissue or onionskin bond, and all tears in margins with bond paper of suitable weight.

2. *Preparation for Sewing*

(*a*) All double leaves, inserts and folded sheets shall be set out with strips of bond paper.

(*b*) Volumes unsuited for oversewing shall be prepared and reinforced for sewing through their folded sections.

3. *Removing Backs*

(*a*) For magazines that are to be oversewed, folds on the back shall be sanded off with a sand wheel or removed by taking a very narrow trim, not more than $\frac{1}{16}$ inch, so as to leave all back margin possible.

(*b*) Magazines that come wire-stitched in bulky "saddle" style, and which have excessively narrow margins, shall be prepared for oversewing by being slit with a knife by hand (instead of being sanded or cut off).

4. *Dividing into Sections*

(*a*) Magazines that are to be oversewed shall be divided into uniform sections, each section not to exceed 0·050 inch in thickness, except flexible pulpy paper which may be in thicker sections not to exceed 0·060 inch each.

(*b*) All sections of magazines in which paper is moderately stiff shall be scored before oversewing. (Extra stiff papers unless hinged shall not be oversewed, but may be sewed through folded sections after necessary reinforcement of folds.)

5. *Endpapers*

(*a*) Endpapers for ordinary magazine-volumes shall be of the types and construction permissible for books, as specified in Part II, Section 5.

(*b*) Endpapers for heavy, bulky or large magazine-volumes shall receive special reinforcement in accordance with their special needs. Materials like those specified for newspaper-volumes shall be used whenever necessary.

6. *Sewing*

(*a*) Most magazines having proper inner margins and suitable paper shall be sewed with thread by oversewing method, either by machine or by hand. If sewed by machine, all sections shall be pasted. As many needles shall be used as possible, providing that this does not bring the sewing closer to the head and tail of the book than $\frac{1}{4}$ inch after trimming.

(*b*) Because of narrow margins, or for flat opening, exceptional magazines shall be sewed through the folded sections. When such sewing is used, all weak folds shall be reinforced with strips of bond

166

paper, loose leaves hinged in, and the sections sewed on four tapes or cords (or more according to height of volume), with linen thread, usually one-on.

(c) Special arrangements, whenever necessary, shall be made with the library as to the sewing or other handling of magazines which are originally bound by the spiral, plastic or similar methods.

7. *Trimming*

All magazine volumes shall be trimmed to sample, or recorded size, where instructed; otherwise as slightly as possible.

8. *Edges*

Edges shall be sprinkled, stained or left plain as instructed.

9. *Gluing, Rounding, Backing and Lining*

(a) Backs of magazines shall be glued with approved flexible glue, well rounded and backed, and lined with Canton flannel extending to within $\frac{1}{4}$ inch of head and tail of volume, and well on to each endpaper (approximately $1\frac{1}{2}$ inches).

(b) Heavy and large volumes shall be reinforced with tough back-lining paper upon the fabric lining.

10. *Covers*

(a) Covers shall be made of heavy-weight starch-filled or pyroxylin-filled buckram, or sateen-base pyroxylin-coated material of a quality at least equal to the standards set forth in Part V of these specifications.

(b) Covers shall be made over hard-rolled binders board, with uniform squares, in a neat and workmanlike manner. The thickness of the board shall be suited to the size and weight of the volume.

(c) The cover material shall be turned in enough to insure adhesion (normally $\frac{5}{8}$ inch is necessary).

11. *Inlays*

All covers shall have an inlay of flexible paper securely attached to the inside of the backbone of the cover. The paper shall be cut the same length as the cover boards, and the approximate width of the back of the magazine after it has been rounded and backed. The paper shall be of a thickness appropriate to the thickness of the cover boards but not less than 0·01 (one hundredth) of an inch.

12. *Casing in*

Magazines shall be cased in with glycol paste, or equal, and pressed between metal-edged boards until thoroughly dry.

13. *Lettering*

(*a*) Lettering shall be done after proper sizing in clear type of a size appropriate to the magazine, in style and position as instructed, using X.X. 23-carat gold deeply impressed to insure long adhesion to the cover.

(*b*) At the option of the library, approved colored foils or inks may be used; but no gold-colored substitute of any kind may be used without the express approval of the library.

(*c*) Binders shall keep necessary records by which uniformity of sets may be maintained.

14. *Protective Lacquering of Backs*

Magazine volumes shall be sprayed or treated with a protective material evenly applied over their lettered backs.

15. *Inspection*

All magazine volumes shall be carefully opened out and critically inspected for defects in binding or errors in lettering.

PART IV. NEWSPAPERS

General Conditions

These specifications include the various methods of binding newspapers which produce a result satisfactory enough to be considered a minimum standard of good construction, workmanship and materials. Some libraries have in the past had newspaper volumes bound by methods or with materials different in some respect, which may not be recommended for general use. In such cases, where the matching of sets is to be continued, these specifications may be used with instructions covering the points of difference. If there are no such specific changes, the binder is to deliver a volume bound in conformity with these specifications in every respect.

These specifications are based on the following assumptions: (1) The library will furnish the binder with the proper editions, complete with all sections. (2) Fresh (unused) copies will be provided by the library wherever possible. (3) Where used copies are provided, specific arrangements, based on estimates whenever possible, should be made as to the amount of mending, restoring and refolding. (4) No clauses are included here on mounting or preserving the pages, as these are special operations, requiring special arrangements.

1. *Preparation for Sewing*

(*a*) Unless instructions are otherwise, newspaper volumes shall be as

168

APPENDIX II

little as possible over 2 inches in thickness, between covers. (Optional—
2 inches is the preferred size for convenience in handling by binder and
reader, and for durability with normal binding methods and materials.
Where volumes cannot logically be arranged in the 2-inch size, volumes
up to $3\frac{1}{2}$ inches in thickness are practical, but should be covered by
special instructions and special estimates.)

(b) All issues shall be carefully collated to detect any damage and to
assure continuity of pages and proper sequence of dates. (The binder
shall not be held responsible for checking whether the editions furnished
are the particular ones desired to be bound or whether all parts of an
issue have been furnished.)

(c) Newspapers that are creased or badly wrinkled shall be straight-
ened out as much as possible by sponging and pressing, the entire
volume being placed between press boards, while the folds are still
damp, and subjected to heavy pressure in a standing press, overnight.

(d) Sections shall be refolded whenever the original fold is crooked
or is so far off-center that it would cause the sewing to encroach
on the print.

(e) Single leaves shall be tipped in, in proper position for their
sewing.

2. *Dividing into Sections*

Because the narrow inner margins or newspapers preclude trimming or sanding preparatory to sewing, lifts (sections) not exceeding
$\frac{1}{8}$ of an inch in thickness (or approximately 24 to 28 leaves) shall be
considered appropriate for sewing.

3. *Endpapers*

(a) Types of endpapers shall be those permitted for books.

(b) In volumes up to 3 inches in thickness, endpapers shall be of
paper, basis 24 by 36 sixty-pound, with a bursting strength (Mullen
tester) of at least sixty points; in thicker volumes a heavier paper of the
same grade shall be used.

(c) Endpapers shall be reinforced with cloth joints of light-weight
buckram, 8-ounce khaki or fabric of equal strength. The cloth
shall be wide enough so that it will extend at least 2 inches beyond the
sewing.

4. *Sewing*

(a) Every newspaper volume shall be sewed in sections either by
oversewing (by hand or machine) or by sewing on cord or tapes. If
tapes are used, they shall not be less than $\frac{1}{2}$ inch wide. In oversewing,

the stitches shall be continued to within 1½ inches from top and bottom. In oversewing by hand, the stitches shall be no farther apart than 1 inch. Newspaper volumes shall not be stitched, nor sawed and tied with thread or cord, nor otherwise fastened clear through.

(b) Sewing shall go through the reinforcing strips of the endpapers, so as to sew them securely to the first and last sections.

5. *Trimming*

Newspaper volumes shall be trimmed as little as possible, and, if necessary to prevent bleeding the print, on their heads only.

6. *Edges*

Edges may be sprinkled, stained or left plain according to instructions.

7. *Gluing, Rounding, Backing and Lining*

(a) Backs of newspapers shall be glued with approved flexible glue.

(b) Rounding and backing shall be adequate, and no more than necessary for the thickness of the volume and the thickness of the covers.

(c) Backs shall be lined with approved lining fabric, extending to within one inch of the head and tail and leaving an extending flap at least 2½ inches wide on each side. An additional lining of two thicknesses of kraft or rag paper, 24 × 36 sixty-pound basis, shall be glued across the back over the fabric lining.

8. *Covers*

(a) Newspaper volumes may be either full-bound, three-quarter-bound, or half-bound. The main cover material shall be heavy-weight buckram or 8-ounce cotton duck.

(b) Covers shall be made over hard-rolled binders board, with uniform squares, and in a neat and workmanlike manner. Boards shall be suited in thickness to the size and weight of the volume: minimum thickness of board for volumes up to 2½ inches thick, and all volumes of tabloid size, must be 0·120 inch; for volumes from 2½ inches up to 3 inches, 0·160 inch; for volumes 3 inches and more, 0·205 inch.

9. *Inlays*

All covers shall have an inlay of flexible paper securely attached to the inside of the backbone of the cover. The paper shall be cut the same length as the cover boards, and the approximate width of the back of the newspaper after it has been rounded and backed. The paper shall be of a thickness appropriate to the thickness of the cover boards, but not less than 0·01 (one hundredth) of an inch.

10. *Casing in*

For heavy volumes, either the laced-on or split-board method of attaching boards shall be used. In either case, the flap of the back-lining shall be glued to (or within the split of) each board and firmly pressed to insure permanent adhesion. Thereafter, the endpapers shall be glued firmly to each board.

11. *Lettering*

(*a*) Lettering shall be done with X.X. 23-carat gold, deeply impressed to insure long adhesion to the cover. (Optional—At the specific instruction of the library, printer's ink or approved foil may be used.) Imitation gold leaf must not be used.

(*b*) Lettering may be done either directly upon the back of the cover or upon a leather label afterwards firmly attached thereto.

12. *Protective Lacquering of Backs*

All lettered surfaces, except duck, shall be sprayed or treated with a protective material.

13. *Inspection*

All newspaper volumes shall be carefully opened out and critically inspected for defects. Leaves shall be especially examined to ascertain if any have failed to be caught into the sewing.

PART V. APPROVED MATERIALS

The joint committee shall hereafter maintain a free testing service available to any library operating its own bindery, and to any binder operating a certified bindery submitting samples of materials represented as meeting the requirements of the minimum specifications, but which have been judged unsatisfactory by the library or bindery.

1. *Thread*

A. When used for machine oversewing thread shall be at least equal to the standard recommended by the manufacturers of the machine for its proper operation.

B. Thread for hand-sewing shall be linen.

2. *Boards*

A. Board quality shall measure up to the specifications of Commercial Standard CS50–34 for solid binders board.

B. The thickness of the board shall be adapted to the size and weight of the volume bound, and shall be between 0·060 inch and 0·205 inch.

3. *Starch-filled Buckram*

A. (*a*) The base fabric shall be made of cotton thoroughly cleaned and free from waste. It shall be evenly woven, the warp yarns being woven in pairs. It shall be free from an excessive number of imperfections of manufacture.

(*b*) The weight of the stripped fabric shall be not less than 7·9 ounces per square yard.

(*c*) The total thread count, including warp and filling, shall be not less than 110 threads per square inch.

(*d*) The breaking strength (by the strip method) shall be not less than 120 pounds per inch for the warp, and 70 pounds per inch for the filling, and not less than 200 pounds per inch for the sum of warp and filling.

B. (*a*) The starch filling (including pigment) shall constitute at least 20 per cent of the total weight of the finished fabric.

(*b*) The filling shall be applied uniformly to both sides.

(*c*) The amount of pigment shall not exceed 15 per cent by weight of the filler.

C. The finished fabric shall be firm enough to resist rub-off to such a degree that the loss by abrasion will not exceed 8 per cent by weight of the fabric when subjected to abrasion for 2 minutes by flint paper 2/0 on a disk 2 inches in diameter making 1,250 r.p.m. under 3 pounds pressure.

4. *Pyroxylin-filled Fabrics*

A. (*a*) The base fabric shall be made of cotton thoroughly cleaned and free from waste. It shall be evenly woven, the warp yarns being woven in pairs. It shall be free from excessive number of imperfections of manufacture.

(*b*) The weight of the stripped fabric shall be not less than 7.9 ounces per square yard.

(*c*) The total thread count, including warp and filling, shall be not less than 110 threads per inch.

(*d*) The breaking strength (by the strip method) shall be not less than 120 pounds per inch for the warp, and 70 pounds per inch for the filling, and not less than 200 pounds per inch for the sum of warp and filling.

B. The dye shall penetrate through the fabric so that both sides shall be equally colored prior to the application of the filling compound (except in the case of "linen" type finishes).

C. Starch-filled fabrics which are also filled or otherwise treated with pyroxylin shall conform to the specifications for pyroxylin-filled fabrics.

D. (*a*) The filling compound shall be uniform and homogeneous, and may be either of the nitro-cellulose or cellulose acetate type.

(*b*) The filling compound shall constitute at least 10 per cent of the total weight of the finished product.

(*c*) The filling compound shall contain no oxidizable oils.

(*d*) The plasticizing material, including oil, if any, shall not exceed 20 per cent by weight of the filling compound.

(*e*) The amount of pigment in the filling compound shall not exceed one-tenth of one per cent by weight of the finished fabric.

E. The pH value, as determined by standard methods, shall be not less than 6·5 and not more than 7·5; but in the case of "acid dyes" it shall be not less than 6·0.

F. The finished cloth shall be so water-proof that it will permit no penetration by water within a period of 10 minutes, as determined by the ring test.

G. The finished cloth shall be so grease-proof that it will permit no penetration by oleic acid within a period of 5 minutes, as determined by the ring test.

H. Firm and lasting adhesion of the fabric to boards and endpapers shall be readily obtainable without special preparation, using regular library bindery methods and adhesives approved in these specifications.

I. The finished fabric shall be firm enough to resist rub-off to such a degree that the loss by abrasion will not exceed 8 per cent by weight of the fabric when subjected to abrasion for 2 minutes by flint paper 2/0 on a disk 2 inches in diameter making 1,250 r.p.m. under 3 pounds pressure.

J. The finished fabric shall be free of marked odor.

K. Colors shall be at least as fast to light as the equivalent colors of starch-filled buckram.

5. *Pyroxylin-coated Fabrics*

A. The drill-base pyroxylin-coated fabrics shall have the following physical characteristics:

(*a*) The weight of the stripped fabric shall be not less than 5·2 ounces per square yard.

(*b*) The thread count per inch shall be not less than 62 in the warp and 36 in the filling.

(*c*) The breaking strength (by the strip method) shall be not less than 75 pounds per inch for the warp and 43 pounds per inch for the filling.

(*d*) The coating compound shall constitute at least 45 per cent by weight of the finished fabric.

B. The sateen-base pyroxylin-coated fabrics shall have the following physical characteristics:

(*a*) The weight of the stripped fabric shall be not less than 8 ounces per square yard.

(*b*) The thread count per inch shall be not less than 100 in the warp and 64 in the filling.

(*c*) The breaking strength (by the strip method) shall be not less than 95 pounds per inch for the warp and 80 pounds per inch for the filling.

(*d*) The coating compound shall constitute at least 35 per cent by weight of the finished fabric.

C. In all pyroxylin-coated fabrics, the dye shall penetrate through so that both sides shall be equally colored prior to the application of the coating.

D. (*a*) The coating compound shall be uniform and homogeneous, and may be either of the nitro-cellulose or cellulose acetate type.

(*b*) The coating compound shall contain no oxidizable oils.

(*c*) The plasticizing material, including oil, if any, shall not exceed 35 per cent by weight of the coating compound.

(*d*) The amount of pigment in the coating compound shall not exceed 30 per cent by weight of the compound.

(*e*) Residual solvents, if any, shall not exceed one-tenth of one per cent by weight of the finished fabric.

E. The pH value, as determined by standard methods, shall be not less than 6·5 and not more than 7·5; but in the case of "acid dyes" it shall be not less than 6·0.

F. The finished cloth shall be so water-proof that it will permit no penetration by water within a period of 10 minutes, as determined by the ring test.

G. The finished cloth shall be so grease-proof, that it will permit no penetration by oleic acid within a period of 5 minutes, as determined by the ring test.

H. Firm and lasting adhesion of the fabric to boards and endpapers shall be readily obtainable without special preparation, using regular library bindery methods and adhesives approved in these specifications.

I. The finished fabric shall be free from marked odor.

J. Colors shall be at least as fast to light as the equivalent colors of starch-filled buckram.

6. *Leather*

Leather shall be guaranteed from injurious acids, and skins so stamped.

7. *Back-lining*

Back-lining shall be Canton flannel napped on one side, having a thread count of 44 in the warp, 42 in the filling, and a breaking strength of at least 42·5 pounds per inch for the warp.

8. *Inlays*

Inlays shall be of a flexible paper of a thickness appropriate to the thickness of the cover boards, but not less than 0·01 of an inch for books and not less than 0·012 for magazines and newspapers. Grains of the paper must be with the length of the inlay.

9. *Reinforcing Fabric*

A. Reinforcing fabric for endpapers shall be of a quality equal to muslin, having a thread count of 72 to 85 in the warp and 60 to 75 in the filling and a breaking strength of at least 51 pounds per inch for the warp and 44 pounds per inch for the filling.

B. In the case of Type Z endpapers, it is permissible to use reinforcing fabrics which, in combination, have a strength equal to that specified in "A".

10. *Endpapers*

A. With the exception mentioned in 9B, endpapers for books and ordinary magazines shall be of a subdued or neutral tint, basis 24×36 sixty-pound, with a bursting-strength (on the Mullen tester) of at least 60 points.

B. In the case of Type Z endpapers, it is permissible to use paper having a bursting strength of less than 60 points for each of the middle leaves.

11. *Gold*

Gold shall be genuine X.X. 23-carat. (Foils and inks are not specified, but shall be such as will insure legible lettering during the life of the binding.)

12. *Glue*

Glue for backs shall be high-grade flexible, equal to flexible glue approved by the Research Department of the Library Binding Institute.

13. *Paste*

Paste for casing in shall be glycol, or an equal non-warp paste.

THE DURABILITY OF NEWSPRINT

ARISING OUT of the consideration given to the preservation and binding of newspapers it was decided to make a survey of the durability of newspaper files over the past hundred years. Durability was the quality sought rather than embrittlement or discoloration.

It was found that representative examples could be selected from the files of *The Times* as follows: 1 January 1856; 1 July 1871; 1 January 1900; 1 January 1918; 3 May 1930 and 1 January 1941. These specimens were representative of fairly broad groups in which no appreciable change in durability could readily be detected.

1 January 1856. Some little embrittlement of corners and 1 to 1½ inches of fore-edge accompanied by slight discoloration which is most strongly marked in opening twelve pages and closing six pages of volume. Discoloration is accompanied by small dotted foxing.

Comment. A strong, rough-textured white paper which handles fairly well and is still legible. The spine is rusting, but if the volume were stored flat and protected by a slip case there would seem to be no reason why it should not last another hundred years.

1 July 1871. Again some embrittlement of corners and edges at opening and closing of volume but not so marked as in previous volume. The foxing is, however, more strongly marked, and the dotting in the previous volume is replaced by sizeable half-inch diameter spots.

Comment. The paper is of a different texture from the paper used 25 years before and presumably includes, for the first time, some esparto. It appears to be lighter in weight, slightly smoother in texture and not quite so strong or durable as the previous paper. The deterioration is slight, and if it were shelved horizontally and protected with a slip case it should last almost as well as the previous volume.

1 January 1900. The first signs of marked physical deterioration begin to occur at about this time, and this volume, although it is only slightly foxed, is generally discoloured and the opening pages are brittle.

Comment. The paper is of a thinner, smoother nature than preceding volumes, and in spite of the deterioration noted above it remains a fairly strong paper in the body of the volume with the page in quite a legible sound condition.

1 January 1918. A poor brittle paper that is breaking down at the beginning of the volume. There is little foxing, but yellowing is marked throughout, and the edges of the pages will not stand a great deal of handling. Deterioration varies markedly from issue to issue.

Comment. The worst of the First World War volumes. The paper is basically of a poor colour and the discoloration has reduced legibility. This volume can be preserved with careful storage and a slip case for anything up to fifty years but permanent preservation will call for substantial and expensive treatment.

3 May 1930. There are already signs of discoloration with the inevitable slight deterioration, but the paper is quite pliable.

Comment. A medium-weight creamy paper that is going to outlive the volume dated 1 January 1918, but does not appear to have the durability of the volume for 1 January 1900.

1 January 1941. This volume is already showing signs of deterioration and discoloration with a tendency towards brittleness, particularly in the opening pages.

Comment. A medium-weight soft paper in spite of the well calendered surface. The poorest paper in the file of *The Times*. Careful storage will prolong its life, but is not likely to give it a life of another fifty years if subjected to a reasonable amount of use.

General comment. Without the use of laboratory techniques such a survey can only serve as a general guide. However, certain facts are known and these are: that the files have been stored vertically for most of their lives; that the library is only half a mile from a gasworks with the inevitable atmospheric contamination produced by such a works; that the files have been fairly well used by the public.

If the complete files were to be shelved horizontally it would take approximately 15 per cent more space, but it would then be possible to provide slip cases for them without any increase in storage space.

Certain of the files of newspapers issued during the Second World War should be given special treatment page by page, if they are to be preserved.

GLOSSARY

Accordion-pleated fold. A method of folding endpapers so that the pleat provides a reinforced hinge at the inner joints of the cover.

Alaska seal. A rarely used bookbinding leather made from sheepskin and finished to give the appearance of sealskin.

Albumen. White of egg used in preparing glair for finishing with gold leaf. A synthetic product is now occasionally used.

All-along. That method of sewing a book which carries the thread from kettle-stitch to kettle-stitch in each section. Also known as *one on* and *one sheet on.*

All-over. A form of design which covers the whole of a side of a binding but it is also used to mean a repetitive design and is often referred to as *diaper.*

Antique. A trade-term for many materials: (i) *paper*—an esparto paper varying in quality from the puffy lightweight to the fairly heavy laid; (ii) *binding*—blind tooling or blocking; (iii) *leather*—a natural finish usually dark brown.

Arming press. Now usually referred to as a blocking press.

Art. A widely used term the connotation of which varies from the best, the unique, in the case of *art binding*, to the artificial in the case of *art gold, art linen, art leather.* Its meaning when applied to paper also varies widely, *art paper* being a coated paper designed for the reproduction of fine half-tones and *art kraft paper* being a paper with an imitation leather finish.

Back. A term which is sometimes used as a synonym for spine but the more careful use would seem to distinguish between the back of the text which is the spine, and the cloth or leather cover of the spine which is the back.

Back lining. The paper used for stiffening inside the back of the covering material. Also called back strip and inlay.

Back margin. See *inner margin.*

Backing. The process of bending over the back of a book after the sections have been glued together so as to form a lip into which the boards may fit.

Backing boards. Wedge-shaped wooden boards usually with metal facings which are used when backing to form the lip and groove. The narrow end of the wedge lies to the fore-edge when in the press.

Backing machine. A machine which is usually combined with the rounding machine and referred to as a *rounder-backer*. It consists of a self-centring heavy roller which applies considerable pressure and shapes the back of the book to take the boards.

Bands. Originally the cords upon which the book was sewn, subsequently the covered cords or other material across the spine of a book, but the term is now applied to the lines which divide the spine into sections, and do not necessarily show the number of tapes or cords.

Basil. A tanned sheepskin making a moderate quality binding leather, and usually produced in dark shades with a natural finish.

Beating. The process by which hand binders flatten and smooth the paper before binding.

Beating stone. A slab usually set in a frame filled with sand for the beating of books.

Bible style. A flexible round-cornered leather binding.

Bleed. When a book has been trimmed down so that the printed page has been cut it is said to be *bled*. Illustrations running to the edge of the page without margin are also said to be *bled*.

Blocking. Impressing a heated block of letters or relief stamp on a surface by means of a blocking press.

Board papers. That part of the endpapers which is pasted down on to the boards.

Boards. (i) Frequently used to mean the front and back cover of a bound or cased book; (ii) the materials used for stiffening the covers of a book; (iii) variously shaped and sized boards used for many processes including backing, cutting, gilding, etc.; (iv) the term *in boards* indicates that the book has had its boards threaded on but has not been covered.

Bolt. The fold in a section usually at the head and fore-edge, but with modern folding, it also occurs at the bottom or tail edge.

Book covers. The covered sides of a book.

Bound flexible. See *flexible binding.*

Broken. A book is said to be broken when it is split through from head to tail.

Broken over. A folding or turning over of plates before insertion in the volume so that they can be turned easily; also called a French guard.

Buckram. A strong cloth made of cotton or linen with a coarse finish.

Bulk. The thickness of the unbound book.

Bundling. The process of fastening in bundles the newly folded sections of a book.

179

Burnish. The gloss produced by the burnisher on the edges or the leather of the book.

Burnisher. Occasionally steel but usually pieces of agate or bloodstone set in a handle.

Calender. A term applied to cloth and paper when it has been rolled and ironed under pressure, and so given a glossy surface.

Calf. A skin that lacks durability, but is occasionally used for so-called luxury editions and was once widely used. Most such leathers tend to break along the joints and rust after quite a short life.

Cap. A special paper envelope fitted over the pages to protect them while the binding is being finished.

Case. The cover when it is made as a unit apart from the book as in publisher's casing and nowadays in most library binding.

Casing: casing-in: case work. The fitting of a book which has already been sewn, rounded and backed into a case.

Catch stitch. See *kettle stitch.*

Cellulose acetate. A substance used in liquid form to coat or fill book cloths with a view to making them oil-proof and water-proof and also used in film form to reinforce book jackets, and produce illustrated covers (q.v.).

Centre tool. A tool used for the centre of a design which in contrast to border tools gives a complete unit of decoration.

Chased edges. See *gauffered edges.*

Cheeks. The inside surfaces of the plates in a press.

Chiffon. A fine open-wove silk fabric used for repairing documents.

Chipboard. A thin board rather like a light-weight mill-board and used for example as a lining board for a leather-bound book.

Clearing-out. Paring away and removing any surplus leather upon the inside of the board prior to pasting down the endpapers.

Cloth. Woven cover material with a heavy filling, and a special finish usually manufactured from cotton in a wide range of colours.

Cloth boards. (i) A binding in which cloth is used as a covering; (ii) boards which are usually equipped with a metal flange at one edge, and are used to form the groove in a French joint when casing.

Cold glue. Synthetic adhesives which do not require heating and which adhere when dried. They are now widely used in place of the conventional flexible glue.

Collate. Bibliographically the meaning is to compare, but in bookbinding it is more loosely used to mean the process of checking the signatures and insertions to ensure that the book is both complete and in the correct order.

Comb. A tool with metal teeth used for distributing the colours in the marbling tray.

Commercial binder. An undertaking which produces cased publisher's editions by machinery.

Compensation guard. Short stubs bound in a volume to compensate for bulky insertions.

Concealed joint. A cloth joint made by reinforcing the fold with fabric so that it cannot be seen in the finished book.

Concertina fold. See *accordion-pleated fold.*

Cords. The material round which the sections of a book are sewn consisting usually of cord made from cotton, hemp or linen.

Corner tools. A pair of tools which give a complete unit of decoration, and are used for a corner design in left- and right-hand corners.

Corners. The outer junction of two edges of a book cover, but it is also used to indicate the leather or other materials used on the corners in half-binding or three-quarter-binding.

Crash. See *mull.*

Creaser. An edged tool usually of steel used for marking the edges of the bands.

Crinoline. An American term for a heavily finished open-weave cloth rather similar to a low grade mull.

Cropped. A book in which the margins have been cut unduly, but not so badly cut that it has been bled.

Crown. The most used size of paper in book production measuring 20 inches by 15 inches and frequently manufactured in double crown 30 × 20 and quad crown 40 × 30. It produces a folio 15 × 10; a quarto 10 × 7½ and an octavo 7½ × 5.

Crushed grain. A grain of leather rolled so that it is flattened.

Cut-edge book. A book of which the edges have been cut by a knife, but this should not be confused with opened (q.v.).

Cut flush. A book which has been cut with a guillotine after the boards have been added, and as a result the boards do not project beyond the leaves of the book.

Cut in boards. A term applied in craft binding to a book which has been cut with a plough after the boards have been laced on.

Cutting press. See *plough.*

Deckle edge. The rough feathery edge produced by the edge of the mould in the hand-making of paper, and now also applied to a similar edge in machine-made paper.

Demy. A size of paper frequently used in book production measuring 22½ inches by 17½ inches. The book sizes are folio 17½ × 11¼; quarto 11¼ × 8¾; and octavo 8¾ × 5⅝.

Doubled. The design is doubled when in placing a tool a second time it is not placed exactly on the first impression.

Doublure. A lining of leather or silk or a rich material inside the cover board.

Drawn on. A method of fastening a cover to a book by gluing it to the spine and to a strip adjoining the spine. It is largely used for paper-covered books.

Dummies. Books made up out of waste or blank sheets to give the appearance of a finished book usually for estimating purposes.

Duodecimo. A book made up of sheets which have been folded into 12 leaves or 24 pages. Usually written as 12mo.

Dutch corner. See *library corner.*

Dutch metal. An imitation gold leaf in sheet and powder form.

Edge-rolled. When the projecting edges of the boards of a book are decorated with a roll they are said to be *edge-rolled.*

Edition binding. The type of binding supplied to publishers when a large number of copies are uniformly bound.

Endpapers. The extra unprinted pages at the beginning and end of the text, a sheet of which is used for pasting down inside the boards. It is loosely used to mean a pair of conjugate leaves one of which is pasted down as a cover lining.

English finish. A finish to bookbinding cloth which gives it an appearance rather similar to linen.

Extra binding. The binding of books with extra care and superior materials sometimes used to distinguish hand binding from casing.

False back. See *hollow back.*

Fanning out. The arrangement of sections or sheets so that each is arranged to project a little along one edge.

Featherweight. A lightweight puffy paper.

Fiddle. To fasten sections by means of cross-stitch, thread going from one section to the next and back again down the length of the spine.

Filled. A fabric of which the interstices are filled with a chemical in order to give the fabric body and the surface a finish.

Fillet. A cylindrical revolving wheel mounted in a wooden handle which is used for impressing lines on a book cover. It is also occasionally used to signify the lines so made.

Finisher. The craftsman who completes the binding by lettering and decorating the covered book.

Finishing press. A small horizontal press for holding a book while it is being tooled.

Finishing stove. A stove used for heating the tools used for finishing.

Flange. Projection on either side of a rounded and backed book.

Flat back. An unrounded book with the back at right angles to the sides.

Flat stitching. The sewing together of single leaves or sections usually by wire through the entire thickness of leaves and sections. Also called flat sewing and side stitching.

Flexible binding. A binding made by sewing round raised bands or cords. It is occasionally used to mean unsewn or "perfect" binding.

Flexible glue. A mixture of animal glue and glycerine or rubber.

Fly leaves. The free leaves in a full endpaper section, but also occasionally used to indicate the leaves next to the covers.

Foil. The leaf used as a substitute for gold and made in a wide range of colours and gold and silver.

Fold sewing. An American term to indicate conventional book sewing by means of which the sections are sewn through the centre fold either by hand or by machine.

Folder. (i) A machine which folds paper and is used in the production of a book; (ii) a bone knife resembling a paper knife and used in a number of forwarding processes.

Folio. A sheet of paper folded once to form two leaves and four pages, and also used in conjunction with a paper size to indicate a book size —foolscap folio $13\frac{1}{2} \times 8\frac{1}{2}$ inches.

Foolscap. A size of paper occasionally used in book production measuring 17 inches by $13\frac{1}{2}$ inches.

Fore-edge. The front or outer edges of the leaves of a book; the edge opposite the main folds of the sections.

Forel. An inferior parchment dressed to look like vellum and made from skivers.

Format. The number of times the printed sheet of a book has been folded to make up a section, but it is also loosely used to indicate the size and shape of a book.

Forwarder. The craftsman who carried out the forwarding.

Forwarding. Those operations between the sewing and the finishing of a book which consist of trimming, rounding and backing, lining up and covering, etc.

Foxed. Books or paper which are stained with rusty spots or patches— the staining is usually attributed to dampness, but it seems likely that impurities in manufacture may combine with sulphur dioxide to produce them.

French corner. A method of reinforcing corners with leather or cloth which is subsequently covered on the outside of the board but can just be seen at the inside corner.

French joint. That type of joint made by keeping the boards a short distance from the spine, so that stronger leather or cloth may be used and thus allow the hinge to work freely.

Front cover. That part of a bookbinding or casing which lies in front of the beginning of the book.

Full-bound. A book wholly covered with leather, but also used to indicate any book bound in one material with the result that it is now usually replaced with the terms full-leather, full-cloth.

Full gilt. A book with all opening edges gilt; also known as gilt edges, and gilt all round. The term is also applied to a spine heavily decorated in gold.

Gathering. The process of collecting the folded sheets in the order in which they are to be bound. The term is also used to mean one section.

Gauffered edge. A book edge, usually gilt, bearing an indented decorative design; also spelt *gauffré, goffered.*

Gilding. The method of burnishing gold on to the edges of a book.

Gilt all round. See *full gilt.*

Gilt edges. See *full gilt.*

Glair. A liquid with a high albumen content used for sizing books preparatory to using gold for finishing and also occasionally used to glaze leather. Sometimes spelt glaire.

Gluing up. The gluing together of the sections of a book at the spine prior to rounding and backing.

Gold cleaner. See *gold rubber*

Gold cushion. A pad covered with rough leather to which the gold-leaf adheres so that it can be easily cut and picked up.

Gold knife. A long, narrow, fairly blunt knife used for cutting gold-leaf.

Gold-leaf. A very thin leaf of pure gold used for finishing.

Gold rubber. A piece of specially made absorbent rubber used to remove the superfluous gold-leaf after gilding, and subsequently sold back to the refiners for the extraction of the gold.

Gouge. A finisher's tool which produces a curved line.

Grain. In paper and board the direction in which the fibres lie, and in leather the surface texture either natural or artificial.

Graining. The use of engraved metal plates or wooden boards which are applied with pressure to produce the grain.

Groove. (i) The space between the back and the board in a French joint; (ii) the depression at the spine edge at the front and back cover.

Guard. (i) Strip of paper or cloth sewn into the book and used to provide a hinge for an inserted map, picture or plate; (ii) a reinforcing strip of paper or cloth fixed to the joint of a conjugate pair of leaves; (iii) strips of paper or card bound into a book to provide an extra-wide spine in order to allow for the insertion of additional material.

Guillotine. Machine used for cutting paper or board with the blade usually operating in a vertical plane.

Gutter. The space between the two printed pages formed by the inner margins.

Half-bound. A book with leather corners and a leather spine, which extends one-quarter of the width of the boards—the remainder of the binding is in contrasting material such as cloth or paper.

Handletters. Single relief letters, figures or ornaments fixed into a handle in contrast to brass type assembled in a pallet. Also called *letter tools.*

Head. That part of a book above the top line of printing or manuscript and occasionally used to indicate the top of the spine.

Head cap. A piece of leather folded over the top of the spine to cap the headband.

Headband. A protective decorative band usually made of threaded silk and either glued or sewn to the spine so that it just projects on the inside edge of the head of the spine.

Hinge. (i) The material that is used to fasten the body of the book to its covers; (ii) a guard that is used to allow the free turning of an inserted single sheet of a book.

Holing. Piercing the boards with a bodkin in order to allow the cords to pass through.

Hollow back. A book bound in such a way that the covering material is fixed at the joints, but not fastened to the spine, and in this way the spine retains its shape when the book is opened. Also called loose back, open back.

Hollow tooling. A design which is outlined usually in gold.

Hooks. The specially designed needles used in book sewing machines.

Illustrated covers. The type of binding which incorporates the original publisher's dust-jacket or cover which is usually protected by or laminated with a plastic film.

Imitation gold. A substitute gold-leaf which is used on inferior binding and casing and tarnishes more quickly than gold-leaf.

Imperfect. A book is imperfect when it is incomplete and the expression is also used for damaged sheets, leaves or plates.

Imperial. A size of paper used in book production measuring 30 inches by 22 inches. The book sizes are folio 22×15; quarto 15×11; and octavo $11 \times 7\frac{1}{2}$.

Imposed. The arrangement of type pages according to a set pattern.

Impregnated. A term used largely in U.S.A. for book cloths treated to give them a moisture-proof finish.

Imprint. In bookbinding (i) the stamping of the mark of ownership at the foot of the spine; (ii) the publisher's name and device stamped at the foot of the spine.

In boards. See *boards.*

Inlaid. A form of design using leather of a different colour or type pasted over or let into the covering leather.

Inlay. See *back lining.*

Inner margin. The margin adjoining the spine of a book.

Inserts. (i) An illustration or map which is printed separately and subsequently bound in; (ii) a leaflet usually a single sheet for advertising purposes which is not an integral part of the book or periodical into which it is inserted.

Inset. Those pages which are produced by cutting a full sheet, and inserting the folded incomplete sheet into the centre of a normal section. Thus an octavo might have a section in twelves which would be made up of a normal section and an inset of fours.

Inside margin. The leather or material which forms a border inside the boards. Also used for inner margins (q.v.).

Interleaving. The process of inserting extra leaves, usually blank, between the normal pages of a book.

Invisible joint. See *concealed joint.*

Jaconet. A term sometimes used to mean a superior type of mull which is used for lining up the spine, and in most publisher's casing it is used together with the endpaper to connect the book to the case.

Japanese tissue. A thin, strong, transparent tissue used for lining damaged sections or pairs of leaves.

Joints. A term with various connotations in bookbinding usually (i) that part of a book cover which hinges at the groove when the covers are opened; (ii) the reinforcing strips of cloth or other material applied to the fold of the endpapers, and occasionally to the first and last section; (iii) the grooves between the boards and the spine.

Kettle stitch. A stitch used in sewing usually at the head and tail of the spine to give the binding firmness by linking the sewing of each section to that of the previous section or sections. Also called *catch-stitch* and *chain-stitch.*

Knocking-down iron. A flat piece of iron with a projection on the underpart by means of which it is secured in a press, and thus gives a firm surface upon which the boards of a book can be laid in order to allow the projecting slips to be hammered flat.

Kraft paper. A strong brown wood-pulp paper now sometimes used in publishers' casing instead of mull to provide a hinge.

Label. A piece of stamped or printed material which is fastened to the spine or front cover of a book.

Lacing-in. The process of threading the slips to which the book is sewn through the pierced boards.

Laid. A paper made with a wire framework mould; as a result such papers have a look-through with a ribbed appearance.

Laid on. A term applied to gold-leaf when it has been applied to a surface before tooling.

Law calf. Tanned uncoloured calfskin.

Lay cords. The loops of cord on the bar of a sewing frame to which the actual sewing cords are fastened. It is now loosely applied to the actual sewing cords.

Laying press. See *lying press.*

Leaf. (i) A part of a folded sheet or section consisting of two pages back to back; (ii) very fine sheets of metal usually gold which are used for finishing.

Leather cloth. A cloth which has been specially treated usually with cellulose nitrate to give the appearance of leather.

Letter tools. See *hand tools.*

Lettering. The process of impressing heated letters through a colouring medium on to leather cloth or similar material.

Levant. A large-grain attractive finish applied to morocco (q.v.).

Library binding. A special type of binding or reinforced casing which is designed to withstand hard wear in a public library, or the actual process of binding books in this way.

Library corner. A book corner made by not cutting the overlap of the cloth, but by turning in this surplus cloth under the two diagonal folds so that the corner is given an extra reinforcement. Also called Dutch corner, round corner.

Limp. A book so bound that the covers are flexible, a result usually achieved by either not using a board for the cover or by using a light pasteboard or card.

Lining paper. Used rather confusingly to mean (i) that paper which is fastened down inside the front board; (ii) the endpapers as a whole and more frequently today as (iii) the strip of thick paper used inside the back of a book either to supplement the covering fabric or occasionally in a heavy book to supplement the reinforcing fabric.

Lining up. The process in library binding which follows the sewing, trimming and rounding and backing, and which consists of gluing and fastening on the spine any reinforcing material.

Loose back. See *hollow back.*

Lying press. A screw-operated wooden press working in a horizontal plane, and used for many hand-binding processes such as backing and finishing, and also used in conjunction with the plough for cutting.

Marbling. The process of floating and combing colours on a medium—usually size—and transferring the resulting design to paper—hence marbled paper, marbled edges.

Margins. The space on a page round the print or writing, and usually referred to as the top or head margin, the outer or fore-edge margin, the tail or bottom margin, and the inner, back or gutter margin.

Marking up. The marking of the divisions on the spine of the unbound book to indicate where the cords and subsequently where the bands are to appear on the finished spine.

Millboard. A strong board made from old rope or cordage, and varying in colour from light to dark browny grey.

Mitred. (i) The type of corner made by cutting off the surplus covering material in order to give a neatly folded corner; (ii) the corner design in which the lines meet without crossing.

Morocco. A superior type binding leather made from goatskin, and also applied to a cloth which is given a grain finish similar to morocco.

Mount. A piece of material to which is affixed a sheet of paper or a plate.

Mull. A loose open-weave muslin-like cotton fabric used on the spines with a sufficient overlap to reinforce the joint in edition and some library binding.

Nipping. A process which applies pressure for a short time, hence a *nipping press.*

Octavo. A book size produced by folding a sheet of paper into eight leaves or sixteen pages.

One on. See *all-along.*

One sheet. See *all-along.*

Onionskin. A thin, translucent glazed paper used for repairing torn pages, etc.

Open back. See *hollow back.*

Opened. A book which has had the fold slit with a paper knife so that it can be read. It should not be confused with cut or cut-edge (q.v.).

Overcasting. See *oversewing.*

Oversewing. The sewing technique by means of which the thread passes through the edge of the section, and then round the back before it is reinserted in the edge again. It is also sometimes applied to the machine technique which sews with thread through the edge of each section often using pre-formed holes. It is also called whip-stitching and overcasting.

Oxford corner. The corner design in which the lines of the design cross in the corners at right angles.

Page. Most usually means one side of the leaf of a book, but can also mean the size of the printed area on one side of a leaf or book.

Pallet. (i) A brass type holder with a wooden handle which the finisher uses for holding and heating the brass letters; (ii) a metal finishing tool usually consisting of a line or ornament suitable for the back of a book.

Pamphlet. A printed work of one section in paper covers, but also used, particularly in America, to mean any paper-covered work of 64 pages or less.

Panel. The space on the back or sides of a book limited by joined lines.

Papering. Pasting down the endpapers.

Parchment. Usually made of sheepskins, but also from goat and calf. It is a thinner skin than vellum, but processed in the same way, and is designed to give a surface suitable for writing and printing.

Paring. The process of thinning down leather or paper.

Paste boards. A material made by pasting sheets of paper together, or occasionally by pulping and remoulding paper, which was much used in early bookbinding until it was replaced by millboard and strawboard.

Paste wash. Paste thinned with water most usually for the purpose of sizing leather.

Pattern. In the binding of sets the pattern is the specimen volume, sample book, or rubbing sent to the binder to ensure uniformity.

Pencil. The fine small camel's hair brush used for glairing.

Perfect. A term used by the Sheridan Company of America for unsewn binding (q.v.)

Pigskin. A leather used for binding. It is often stated to be both strong and durable, but, in fact, it appears to deteriorate quickly.

PIRA tested. A test devised by the Printing Industry Research Association to ascertain the resistance of leather to sulphuric acid.

Plastic binding. A method of producing a flat-opening binding much used for commercial catalogues and occasionally trade journals and books. It consists of a plastic cylinder with projecting tongues which fit through slots near the binding edge and are then curled within the cylinder.

Plate. An illustration printed on paper different from that of the text.

Plough. A wooden frame fitted with a knife and used by hand binders to cut the edges of a book which is held in a lying press.

Polisher. A steel or bone implement used for polishing leather.

Portfolio. A case for holding loose papers, illustrations, engravings, etc., and made by fastening together at the back a cover with deep flaps, and a conventional cover—these covers are then usually fastened at fore-edge and head and tail by tapes.

Preliminary matter. The printed matter including title-page, foreword, list of chapter-headings, etc. which precedes the actual text of the book. It is often referred to as *prelims.*

Press. A generic term for a wide variety of bookbinding machines which are used for holding or pressing.

Pressing board. A wooden board used between backs when lying in a press under pressure.

Proof. The leaves of a book left uncut by the bookbinder in order to show that the book has not been cut beyond the margins planned by the typographer.

Publisher's binding. The casing of a book as provided by the publisher.

Pulled. A book which has been reduced to separate sections prior to rebinding.

Pyroxlin. A term used in U.S.A. for a wide range of substances used to fill or coat cloth, and designed to give such cloth added strength and make it stain- and water-resistant.

Quarter binding. A binding with leather back and cloth-bound sides, or occasionally, with cloth back and paper sides. Correctly bound the material used for the back should also cover one-eighth of the width of the boards.

Quarter-joint case. A method of binding invented by PATRA so that the book opens flat. The unattached cloth at the joint between the board and the back liner is one-quarter of the total thickness of the book.

Quarto. A book size produced by folding a sheet of paper into four leaves or eight pages.

Quire. (i) 24 sheets; (ii) a term now rarely used for a section and hence (iii) a book in sheets is occasionally said to be in quire.

Raised bands. The bands on the back of a book which have been raised by means of nippers.

Reback. The process of fitting a new back-strip without disturbing the boards or renewing the material covering the boards.

Recase. A book re-bound with its original case.

Recover. The process of merely recovering and refinishing a previously bound book.

Recto. The right-hand page which usually bears the odd pagination. It is also used to indicate the front of a single printed sheet.

Register. (i) The complete list of signatures appearing in a complete book, and occasionally given at the end of early printed books (ii) the positioning of the print on a page in relation to the print on other pages of the book. It is said to be in register when the print area coincides and out of register when it does not so coincide.

Reinforced. Binding that has been strengthened to meet public library use, and usually consists of a cloth-lined hinge and spine or special stitching.

Reinforced endpaper. An endpaper which is strengthened with fabric at the hinge and thus given added strength.

Restored. The process of rebinding in such a way as to retain the original covering material and occasionally the boards. It is used for old bindings.

Ridge. See *flange*.

Roan. Sheepskins usually tanned in sumach.

Roll. See *fillet*.

Rolling machine. The machine used for pressing the printed book between two rollers in order to flatten it. The machine does the work of beating in the hand technique. It is also called a nipping press or smasher.

Rotary cutter. A circular blade revolving at high speed for the precision cutting of board and card.

Rough edge. An uncut edge.

Rough gilt. A book which has its edges gilt before it is sewn.

Round corner. See *library corner*.

Rounding. The process of making a spine convex.

Rounding and backing. The combined operation of rounding and providing a flange for the cover boards either by hand hammering or by a rounding and backing machine.

Roundlet. A small fillet.

Rubber binding. An earlier term for unsewn binding.

Rubbing. A copy of the pattern and lay-out of the finishing of a binding by rubbing with black lead or a similar substance, a piece of strong thin paper which is laid over the binding.

Run-up. A cover with decorative unbroken lines running from top to bottom.

Russia leather. Originally a calf tanned in willow bark, scented with birch oil and dyed red. Today a term applied to a wide variety of inferior leathers.

Saddle stitching. Stitching sections with thread or wire through the fold by placing the section over the apex of the triangle or saddle.

Sagging. The pulling forward of the leaves of a book so that the back tends to become concave.

Sanding. The roughening of the spine by machine sometimes used in roughening the spine in the unsewn process, and also applied to the edges in order to clean them.

Sawn-in. A book in which the cords lie in sawn grooves in the spine.

Seal. A hard-wearing leather with an attractive appearance.

Section. A group of conjugate pairs of leaves designed for sewing as one unit most usually the folded printed sheet of a book.

Self cover. A pamphlet cover of the same material as the body of the pamphlet.

Semée. A heraldic term used to indicate the repetition of a small design at regular intervals over a binding.

Set-out. An insert is said to be set-out when it is mounted on a guard in such a way that it unfolds flat.

Sewing. The process of fastening pairs of leaves to make sections which are then fastened together by means of the same thread to complete the book.

Sewing cords. The cords, tapes or other material round which the sections of a book are sewn.

Sewing frame. A piece of wooden equipment consisting of a flat horizontal wooden platform and two threaded uprights supporting a cross-bar. The tapes or cords to which the sections of the book are sewn are fastened between this cross-bar and the platform.

Sewing keys. Metal keys which retain the cord or tapes in the platform of the sewing frame.

Sewing press. See *sewing frame.*

Sewing stick. A heavy stick of wood used by a sewer to beat down and compress the sewn sections of a book.

Sheet. The piece of paper on which the pages of a book are printed, and which when folded becomes a section or part of a section.

Side stitching. See *flat stitching.*

Signature. The small letters and figures which appear at the foot of the first page of each section to serve as a guide to the order of the sections. It is also used as a synonym for section.

Size. A liquid bond applied to a book cover to serve as a medium for finishing.

Skiver. A split sheepskin which is usually brightly dyed.

Slipcase. An open-fronted box made of cloth-covered board and designed to hold and protect a book or books.

Slips. The projecting pieces of cord or tape which are fastened to the covers of a book.

Smasher, or smashing press. A machine which squeezes the backs of thread-sewn books to predetermined regular thicknesses.

Solander case. A carefully made box with a hinged or detachable lid used to hold and protect books, pamphlets and papers.

Spine. The back of the text which normally carries the tapes or cords, or the covered back of the book on which the title is lettered.

Spiral binding. The method of binding by which the inner margins of the individual pages are pierced with holes, and then bound together with a spiral of non-rusting wire.

Split boards. Two boards fastened together to make a cover board, the tapes or cords being glued between them.

Sprinkled edges. The edges of a book that have been sprinkled with colour.

Square corner. A simple type of bound corner in which a piece is taken out of the covering material so that the cloth can be simply turned in to produce an overlapping corner without folds.

Squares. The projection of the boards beyond the text.

Stabbing. See *flat stitching.*

Stained edges. The edges of a book which have been brushed or sprayed with colour to prevent them from showing dirt.

Stamp. An intaglio or relief design in metal which is heated, and then impressed on the cover or spine of a book by means of a blocking press.

Stamping press. See *blocking press.*

Standing press. A heavy fixed press working in a vertical plane and used for the pressing of books.

Started. Applied to a book in which a section or sections have pulled away from the spine and so project at the fore-edge.

Stitching. The process of fastening together a section or a complete work by passing wire or thread through from the front to the back of the text. It includes such processes as side stitching and saddle stitching, and is in contrast to sewing.

Straight grain. A term applied to leather that has been damped and rolled or boarded so that the grain of the leather lies in straight lines.

Stub. See *guard* (i).

Sumach. The extract from an African shrub used in the tanning of leather.

Super. See *mull.*

Tail. The bottom of the page or spine of a book.

Tailband. A similar protecting decorative band to a headband, but less frequently used and projecting inside the tail of the spine.

Tapes. The sections of a book may be sewn to tapes, and the term is also used for the cords which may also serve the purpose of tapes.

T.e.g. Top-edge gilt.

Three-quarter-bound. A book bound in a similar way to a half-bound book except that the leather on the spine is carried farther across, three-eighths, or thereabouts, of the width of the boards with proportionately larger corners.

Thrown out. An insert is thrown out when it is mounted to a page-size guard in such a way that when it is unfolded it lies flat outside the text.

Ties. Decorative silk or leather cords occasionally fixed to the boards of large books in order to prevent sagging.

Tight back. The spine of such a binding is fastened to the back so that it does not become hollow when open. It is normally used for leather-bound books.

Tipping. The method of fastening an insert in a book by pasting a narrow margin at the binding edge (without the use of a guard).

Title piece. A label carrying the title of the work usually in contrasting colour and of a different material to the front board on which it is fastened.

Tooling. The impressing by hand of a heated tool on leather or some other covering material.

Tools. The implements bearing a relief design in metal and used when heated for impressing a design on covers.

Tooth burnisher. A tool with a curved end used for burnishing the edges of a book prior to marbling.

Trimmed edges. The edges of a book which have been lightly cut without opening the bolts.

Trindles. Thin metal bifurcated plates used in hand-binding to flatten and support the back of the book so that it may be cut by the plough.

Turn-in. The covering material that is turned over from the outside to the inside of the board to form a narrow margin. A turning-in-machine is used for this purpose in mechanical binding.

Turned grain. Leather that has been damped and the grain of which has then been turned with a burnisher.

Turning-up. The flattening out and clamping of the rounded back so that it may be cut by the plough.

Two sheets on. The method of sewing books in which two sections are treated as one by passing the thread from one section to another. It is used to sew books of many sections so that the swelling at the spine is minimized.

Tying up. A process of tying a covered book in order to ensure that the leather on the spine adheres firmly.

Typeholder. A metal tool designed to hold and heat letters before they are impressed on the covering material. Also called pallet.

Uncut. Edges which are not trimmed and so not reduced below the original size when the book is re-bound.

Unopened. A book of which the bolts have not been cut to enable the book to be read.

Unsewn binding. The process of binding which consists of trimming off the folds, and so reducing the book to individual leaves which are then fastened together by a film of adhesive.

Varnish. A special type of varnish is used by bookbinders to give a finish and act as a preservative.

Vellum. An untanned skin, usually calf, which is exposed to lime and polished with pumice to give it a hardwearing, smooth white finish.

Verso. The left-hand page which usually bears the even pagination. It is also used to indicate the back of a single sheet.

Visible joint. A cloth hinge which is pasted down on top of the endpapers to reinforce them.

Warping. A distortion of the covers usually caused by over-damping or hasty pressing.

Waste. (i) Excess paper or leather cut off by the binder; (ii) surplus advertisements or paper not required for binding; (iii) old books or excess sheets used for lining.

Whipping or whip stitching. See *oversewing.*

Whole-binding. See *full-bound.*

Wire stitching. The process of stitching a book with wire stitches either using the side stitch or the saddle stitch.

Witness. See *proof.*

Wove. A paper made by using a woven wire sieve as a mould. The method gives a fairly even mottled look-through as opposed to the ribbed appearance of laid paper.

Yapp. A soft leather binding of which the edges project beyond the text. Hence the term yapped is applied to any covering material such as paper or pasteboard which projects beyond the text.

Select Bibliography

GENERAL

Coutts, H. J. *and* Stephen, G. A. *Manual of library bookbinding: practical and historical.* Libraco, 1911.

Diehl, E. *Bookbinding: its background and technique.* New York, Rinehart, 1946. 2 vols.

Feipel, Louis N. *and* Browning, Earl W. *Library binding manual . . .* Chicago, American Library Association, 1951.

Jennett, S. *The making of books.* Faber, 1951.

Philip, Alex J. *The business of bookbinding for librarians, publishers, students, binders and the general reader.* 2nd ed. Gravesend, Philip, 1935. Specimens of leather, leather-cloth and cloth included.

United States Government Printing Office. *Theory and practice of bookbinding.* Washington, Public Printer, 1950. (United States Government Printing Office apprentice training series—orientation period.)

Whetton, Harry *ed. Practical printing and binding: a complete guide to the latest developments in all branches of the printer's craft.* Odhams Press, 1946.

HISTORY OF BOOKBINDING

Harrison, Thomas. "Early European and Persian bindings: an analytical comparison." *Paper and Print,* vol. 21, no. 2, pp. 130–134.

Harthan, John P. *Bookbindings in the Victoria and Albert Museum.* H.M.S.O., 1950. (Victoria and Albert Museum illustrated booklet No. 2.)

Hobson, G. D. *English binding before 1500.* Cambridge, C.U.P.; 1929. (Sandars lectures series).

THE RAW MATERIALS OF BOOKBINDING—PAPER

Clapperton, Robert Henderson. *Modern paper making.* 3rd ed. Oxford, Blackwell, 1952.

Craig, F. A. "Practical paper making." *Paper and Print.* A well-illustrated series of articles as follows:
1. Introduction, vol. 22, no. 3, pp. 245–250.
2. The constituents of paper, vol. 22, no. 4, pp. 389–392.

Gilmour, S. Carter, *ed. Paper: its making, merchanting and usage; the paper merchant's textbook. . . .* National Association of Paper Merchants. In conjunction with Longmans, Green, 1955.

The Library Association. *The durability of paper: report of the special committee set up by the Library Association.* London, The Library Association [1930].

Overton, John. *Paper for book production.* Cambridge University Press for the National Book League, 1955. 16 pp. Bibliog. (The Book—Number Three).

THE RAW MATERIALS OF BOOKBINDING—CLOTH, LEATHER, LEATHER-CLOTH

[Clyne, Anthony]. "Well dressed literature: morocco and calf." *Paper and Print,* vol. 21, no. 1, p. 48.

The Holliston Mills, Inc. *The making of bookbinding fabrics; being an illustrated story showing the various processes required to transform raw cotton into a finished bookbinding fabric.* Norwood, Massachusetts, The Holliston Mills, Inc. [n.d.]

Hughes, G. Bernard. "Old English parchment." *Paper and Print,* vol. 21, no. 3, pp. 210–216.

A brief historical survey of the use of parchment, and a description of the present-day method of manufacturing parchment.

Innes, R. Faraday. "The preservation of bookbinding leathers." *Library Association Record,* vol. 52, no. 12, pp. 458–461.

Middleton, Bernard C. "Deterioration of bookbinding leather." *Paper and Print,* vol. 23, no. 3, pp. 326–330.

"Synthetic resins enhance today's bookbindings." *Textile World,* August 1945, pp. 104–105.

"Test-tube 'leathers' for bookbinding and how they grew." *Bookbinding and Book Production,* March 1953, pp. 42–43, and April 1953, pp. 39–40.

An outline of the various coated fabrics and plasticized papers available in U.S.A. as a substitute for book cloths.

BOOKBINDING BY HAND

Cockerell, Douglas. *Bookbinding, and the care of books; a textbook for bookbinders and librarians.* 5th ed. Pitman, 1953.

Gould, F. C. "Craft bookbinding." *British Printer,* September–October 1950, pp. 31–32.

Mason, John. *A practical course in book-crafts and bookbinding.* London, Batsford [1935].

Middleton, Bernard C. "Book endpapers and their attachment." *Paper and Print,* vol. 23, no. 4, pp. 431–436.

Middleton, Bernard C. "Further notes on the hand sewing of books." *Paper and Print*, vol. 24, no. 2, pp. 161–164.
Middleton, Bernard C. "Notes on the art of covering with leather." *Paper and Print*, vol. 25, no. 3, pp. 316–321; vol. 25, no. 4, pp. 430–435.
Middleton, Bernard C. "Notes on the hand sewing of books." *Paper and Print*, vol. 24, no. 1, pp. 45–48; vol. 24, no. 2, pp. 161–164.
Middleton, Bernard C. "Scale in bookbinding." *Paper and Print*, vol. 23, no. 2, pp. 202–206.
Town, Laurence. *Bookbinding by hand*. Faber. 1952.

THE MAKING OF A BOOK

Leighton, Sir Robert. "Modern bookbinding methods." *British Printer*. December 1951, vol. LXIV, no. 381, pp. 56–58.
Waters, Charles, "Modern bookbinding—edition binding." *Paper and Print*.

A series of seven articles each of which is devoted to one aspect of edition binding as follows:
1. Edition binding, vol. 21, no. 4, pp. 326–330.
2. Folding, vol. 22, no. 1, pp. 45–48.
3. Endpapering, vol. 22, no. 2, pp. 141–144.
4. Sewing to casing-in, vol. 22, no. 3, pp. 262–265.
5. Lining, vol. 22, no. 4, pp. 385–386.
6. Casemaking—hand, vol. 23, no. 1, pp. 79–82.
7. Casing-in, vol. 23, no. 2, pp. 158–159.

COMMERCIAL LIBRARY BINDERIES

Riley, B., and Co., Ltd. *A modern library bindery*. Huddersfield, Riley and Co., Ltd. 1935.
Stratton, J. B. "Libraries and commercial binderies." *Library Trends*, vol. 4, no. 3; January, 1956, pp. 301–311.

THE LIBRARY BINDERY

Baatz, Wilmer H. "Public library binderies: their duties and supervision." *Bookbinding and Book Production*. May, 1952.
Drewery, Robert Forrester. *Library binderies*. The Library Association, 1950.
Kingery, R. E. "The bindery within the library." *Library Trends*, vol. 4, no. 3; January, 1956, pp. 291–300.

Tauber, M. F., *and others. Technical services in libraries.* . . . New York, Columbia University Press, 1954.
Chapter XVII. The conservation of library material: the bindery within the library and the handling of special materials.

BINDING OF SPECIAL CLASSES OF MATERIAL

Cockerell, S. M. "The binding of manuscripts," *in* Lamb, C. M., *ed. The calligrapher's handbook.* Faber, 1956. pp. 199–223.
Ditzion, Sidney, and Norman, Leverett. "Problems of periodical and serial binding." *Library Trends,* vol. 4, no. 3; January, 1956, pp. 248–258.
United States. Library of Congress—Division of Maps. *Maps; their care, repair and preservation in libraries,* by Clara Egli Legear. Washington, Library of Congress, 1949.

THE REPAIR AND CARE OF BOOKS

Adams, R. G. "Librarians as enemies of books." *Library Quarterly* vol. 7, pp. 317–331, July 1937.
Baughman, Roland. "Conservation of old and rare books." *Library Trends,* vol. 4, no. 3; January, 1956, pp. 239–247.
Harrison, Thomas. "The Solander book box portfolio and its affinities." *Paper and Print,* vol. 2, no. 1, pp. 26–30.
Langwell, W. H. "The permanence of paper records." *The Library Association Record,* vol. 55, no. 7; July 1953, pp. 212–215.
Lawrie, L. G. "Some notes on the chemicals used in the restoration and repair of books and documents." *Library Association Record,* 1944, vol. 46, pp. 114–117.
Lydenberg, Harry Miller, and Archer, John. *The care and repair of books.* 3rd ed. New York. R. R. Bowker. 1945.
Middleton, Bernard C. "Notes on the repair of books." *Paper and Print,* vol. 24, no. 3, pp. 332–339.
"Mildew—its cause and cure." *Bookbinding and Book Production.* February 1950, p. 44.
"Mildew on books." *Library Journal.* 1946, pp. 1094–1096.
Peacey, P., and Barlow, F. "Urea-formaldehyde resin as a vehicle for semi-permanent insecticidal and fungicidal coatings on bookbindings and bookcases." *Journal of Documentation,* 1953, vol. 9, no. 3, pp. 157–168.
Plenderleith, H. J. *The preservation of leather bookbindings.* London, The British Museum; Cambridge University Press, 1946.

"The preservation and repair of old books." *British and Colonial Printer,* vol. 148, no. 1160; 23 February 1951, pp. 192–200.

Unwin, Max, and Middleton, Bernard C. "An improved leather dressing." *Museums Journal,* vol. 51, no. 3; June 1951, pp. 69–70.

ADMINISTRATION

Howarth, R. "In search of a popular binding." *Librarian,* February, 1952, vol. 41, no. 2, pp. 21–23.

Lathem, E. C. "Some personnel considerations for binding and conservation services." *Library Trends,* vol. 4, no. 3; January, 1956, pp. 321–334.

UNSEWN BINDING

Clough, E. A. "Perfect binding: a new development." *Library Association Record,* October 1949, vol. 16, pp. 310–312.

"Getting the most out of notch binding." *Bookbinding and Book Production,* vol. 56, no. 6, pp. 53–54.

Knutsson, Knut. " 'The perfect binding' metoden." *Biblioteksbladet,* vol. 35, no. 5, pp. 242–244.

National Adhesives. "Hot melt adhesive." *Printing Equipment Engineer,* 1950, vol. 81, no. 1, p. 68.

RECENT DEVELOPMENTS

Barrow, W. J. "The Barrow method of laminating documents." *Journal of Documentary Reproduction,* June, 1939, vol. 2, pp. 147–151.

Barrow, W. J. *Manuscripts and documents: their deterioration and restoration.* Virginia, University of Virginia Press, 1955.

A detailed study of the author's method of preserving documents by laminating them with cellulose acetate.

Hummel, R. O., and Barrow, W. J. "Lamination and other methods of preservation." *Library Trends,* vol. 4, no. 3; January 1956, pp. 259–268.

Nixon, H. M. "The lamination of paper documents with cellulose acetate foil." *Archives,* Michaelmas, 1949, no. 2. pp. 32–36.

Oswin, C. R. *Protective wrappings.* Cam Publications, 1954.

Scribner, B. W. *Protection of documents with cellulose acetate sheeting.* Issued 20 December 1940. Washington, Government Printing Office, 1941. (National Bureau of Standards Miscellaneous Publication M. 168.)

INDEX